YOU HAVE A BOOK IN YOU

Also by Mark Victor Hansen

Books

Chicken Soup for the Soul series—254 different books in print

The One Minute Millionaire

Cracking the Millionaire Code

Cash in a Flash

How to Make the Rest of Your Life the Best of Your Life

The Aladdin Factor

Dare to Win

The Richest Kids in America

The Miracle of Tithing

The Power of Focus

The Miracles in You

Out of the Blue

Master Motivator

You Are the Solution

You Have a Book in You

Speed Write Your Personal Life Story

Speed Write Your First Fiction Book

Speed Write Your Nonfiction Book

Speed Write Your Mega Book Marketing Plan

Speed Write Your First Play

Speed Write (and Deliver) Your Killer Speech

Speed Write Your Amazing Publishing Plan

Speed Edit Your First Book

Visualizing Is Realizing

Dreams Don't Have Deadlines

Audios

How to Think Bigger than You Ever Thought You Could Think

Dreams Don't Have Deadlines

Visualizing Is Realizing

Sell Yourself Rich

Chicken Soup for the Soul series

The One Minute Millionaire

Cracking the Millionaire Code

YOU HAVE A BOOK IN YOU

Make Money with YOUR Story

MARK VICTOR HANSEN

MEDIA

Published 2020 by Gildan Media LLC
aka G&D Media
www.GandDmedia.com

Front cover design by David Rheinhardt of Pyrographx

Interior design by Meghan Day Healey of Story Horse, LLC

Library of Congress Cataloging-in-Publication Data is available upon request

ISBN: 978-1-7225-0261-4

10 9 8 7 6 5 4 3 2 1

CONTENTS

PREFACE

Be Ye Inspired to Write!

You're reading this right now because you have an awareness inside that there is a book in you that needs to come out. Perhaps you have many books to share with the world. Writing is a deeply and profoundly inspirational experience for the writer and ultimately for the readers. Books have the ability to inspire in many dimensions, and book writing can create excellence in thought, giving you an ever higher experience of life and living.

Your future is created by being passionately on-purpose about something. Your purpose of being alive is to create and contribute. Writing is inspired creation at its best, and when done in the spirit of excellence, leaves a great and lasting contribution.

Within you now is the ability to write things you never dreamed possible and to serve greatly with love. Writing your book will be an unforgettable learning experience.

Writing is a wonderful way to help you become all that you can be.

Only you have the ability to write your book. Contained herein is perhaps the magic elixir to stimulate you to do it.

Everyone is capable of expressing their unique experiences and understanding through the art of writing. I suspect you have special dreams, understandings, and visions you need to share, or you wouldn't have chosen this book. When you share the wisdom you have locked deep inside of you, you have the potential to change the world.

Maybe someone has told you, "You ought to write a book." Or you've thought it yourself: "I know that this idea is worthy of becoming a book! And I'm the one to do it." That is the perfect place from which your ideas and your talents start to bloom. As you take the first step and your ability to write and clearly express your thinking grows and develops, you'll be energized to keep going. A feeling of awe and wonder will come as you put your ideas and thoughts into form and see them begin to come to life.

A bicycle can only balance if it is moving forward. You as a writer have to keep writing to balance and continue moving ahead on your writing journey.

Connect with your potential fans early. Ask for feedback from friends and get support from the beginning. As your writing grows, you will start to create your own fan base. Your fans will potentially last far into the future, so remember to keep talking to them and also to keep a database.

I am forever reading the brilliance of the ages, written hundreds and thousands of years ago—the works of Plato, Mark Twain, Shakespeare, the apostle Paul, and the stories of leaders like Alexander the Great or Genghis Khan. All departed from physical form long ago but have left us their wisdom contained in the pages of books.

As you move through the writing journey and your book starts to get read, you'll realize that you have the power to influence through your writing. Maybe you'll find opportunities to speak on stages to further illuminate your readers and fans.

Eventually your book could grow into an enterprise of writing and giving speeches and seminars. From there, even more opportunities can blossom, such as offers to speak at universities. I have been given ten honorary doctorates from different universities, which has been a delightful way to leverage my platform and share my message.

Best of all, through your book, you are leaving a printed legacy that will last for all time. Your descendants into many generations will revel in reading their ancestor's work. That's an inspirational legacy worth leaving.

Writing offers more opportunity now than ever in history. Of the 7.8 billion people living on planet earth, approximately 4 billion are literate. My goal is to get everyone to be able to read, write, communicate, and think cooperatively into ever better tomorrows. Books connect minds that are far-flung in place and time, bringing new understandings and illumination and potentially fame and fortune to the author.

For the first time, I am sharing with you my insider's story. I hope it inspires you to release your potential for writing greatness. The writer's challenges and opportunities have never been greater, so roll up your sleeves and get ready to enter the exciting world of authorship.

Writing is an exciting and inviting journey. It can make you better, smarter, and wiser. With marketing prowess, it can also make you vastly richer. Writing books has given me a lifetime of wonderful experiences. I hope it does the same for you. Happy writing!

AUTHOR'S NOTE

I hope and believe the book you're about to read will be much more than words printed on a page. I want this book to be part of an organic process that will encompass many great books by many thousands of authors.

For that to happen, the information in this book will need to continually change and improve based on information from you, the readers and writers. What worked for you in these pages? What didn't work? What would you add or take out?

Please let me know your thoughts at my website, reception@markvictorhansen.com, or by dropping me a note at this address:

Mark Victor Hansen

P.O. Box 27618

Scottsdale, AZ 85255

Additionally, I want you to give me your email address so I can keep you up-to-date on new information, seminars, podcasts, my writings, other great works that you or my students write, and marketing breakthroughs that will help you make your enterprise grow easily, with less effort, and potentially more profitably.

Books are the wealth of the world. Writing them can make you rich. YOU get paid for the quality and quantity of your writing and book marketing abilities. Books are fun at every level, for me and I hope for you. It is easier to work at something you totally enjoy. Writing is definitely my right livelihood and perhaps yours too.

Authorship gives you pride, respect, and the appreciation of adoring readers. It also brings credibility and authority.

Books are extraordinary door openers. They can improve your life and lifestyle.

Books can be written by you alone or with a coauthor, or they can be ghostwritten by someone else.

Books are needed on absolutely every subject. They can be researched fairly easily and can be created inexpensively with paper and pen or on a computer.

Books can be self-published or distributed through a publishing house.

Book publishing—and profit—is as easy as uploading your report, article, chapter, paper, or full manuscript online on your website. You pick the price, and sales commence immediately.

Book distribution has become available to everyone with the acquisition of an ISBN number.

Books have made fortunes for many. J. K. Rowling, author of the Harry Potter books, is the richest woman in Britain thanks to her writing.

Books can enable you to work as a reporter or journalist. For his classic work *Think and Grow Rich,* Napoleon Hill interviewed the five hundred most important men and women of his era. He sold 100 million books, made himself a fortune, and helped our country climb out of the Great Depression.

Before that, Wallace Wattles helped readers emerge from the depression of the 1890s with his classic book *The Science of Getting Rich.* Books have immense potential impacts. That's why I encourage you to write and keep on writing.

Books are your sacred creations, your babies. Creating a book helps you to grow, develop, manifest your fullest potential, and fulfill your destiny. When you look at obituaries, after a persons name and age, comes the book(s) they wrote before any other listings.

Books make the world work. They change your world and your reader's world.

Books last forever. They leave a lasting legacy.

Books enable you to serve greatly with love. They are also fun to create.

Books are like exercise: long after you're done, you still glisten from the effort.

Books travel around the world and invite you along for the ride.

Books help people conquer their fears, be excited about life and living, solve their problems, and improve their circumstances.

Books are inclusive; they exclude no one. Everyone is better off, and no one is left out. Entrepreneur Jim Rohn said, "If you can read and don't, you are no better off than someone who cannot read." Recently Dr. Peter Diamandis's X Prize was just won in Tanzania, where children in forty villages learned to read their native language and English in one and half years—forever changing and improving their lives. Dr. Diamandis, Elon Musk, founder and funder of this X Prize, and I believe that in this decade 4 billion nonreaders will gain the advantage of learning to read, write, and communicate effectively. That could more than double the amount of books sold.

Books can become businesses that create empires. Dale Carnegie's best-selling book *How to Win Friends and Influence People* created a worldwide training empire that grosses over $50 million each year.

Books will introduce you to the most wonderful, helpful, insightful, wise, and leading-edge people in the world.

Books impact lives profitably and permanently. They are a path from one head and heart to another. They connect us all.

Books are your way to a potential fortune.

Book authorship is a magnificent endeavor. Books are a force multiplier as your messages expand outward into the world.

Books stimulate your thinking and the thinking of your readers. They change feelings and consciousness and create new futures and possibilities.

Books advance the cause of freedom. Harriett Beecher Stowe's *Uncle Tom's Cabin* inspired President Abraham Lincoln to become the visionary leader of emancipation. In 1862 President Lincoln issued the Emancipation Proclamation, which is still expanding freedom for ever more people here and around the world.

The best book of all time hasn't yet been written. So *you* have to write it!

INTRODUCTION

This is the business we have chosen.

—The Godfather, part two

That's a famous line from one of the most powerful movies ever made. The script for that film was written by Mario Puzo—who also, of course, wrote the script for the first Godfather film as well as the novel on which it's based. Mario Puzo had a lot of great things to say about writing, so we'll be referring to him and other writers throughout this book. But here at the start I want to focus on one specific word in that quote above.

The word is *business*. When you start to write a book, you're doing more than just punching keys on your keyboard. You're entering the book business, and like every other business, it has many different elements. I want to you to be 100 percent successful in dealing with all those elements.

Sigmund Freud said that people write books for three reasons: fame, love, and money.

So let's make it happen!

But first let me repeat: you're not just writing a book. You're starting a commercial enterprise, which includes marketing, finances, and all the other facets of a profit-making enterprise. The book business requires time and effort, and above all, information. Without information, you can finish a manuscript, but you may also be the only person who ever reads it. I am here to make sure you have all the tools you need to not let that happen!

One more thing . . .

Maybe part of you thinks there's an easier way to achieve those three enticing goals of fame, money, and love. For example, you may be wondering why you can't just start a podcast or a blog and update it every couple of days.

As we'll discuss, you can—and should—start a podcast or blog, but the foundation of your business must be your book. Your book will validate you as a real writer, not just in your reader's mind, but in your own mind too. A book shows you're serious. You've paid the price and jumped through all the hoops required to get it out into the world. Everyone can respect, admire, and appreciate that.

Plus, once your book is in the world, there's no limit to where it can go or the influence it can have. Nothing can change people's lives like a book. Thousands of stories illustrate that fact.

By the way, writing a book can change *your* life as well. My friend Og Mandino wrote *The Greatest Salesman in the World*, a little book that happens to be an all-time best seller. But before he was a writer, Og had a serious alcohol problem. He couldn't be successful at anything. He even thought about ending his life, but fortunately he wasn't successful at that either.

Og was living in New Hampshire, where the winters are about as cold as you can imagine. One day, just to escape the miserable weather, he visited the library. He sat down and found a book on the table in front of him. It was called *The Success System That Never Fails*. The author was the late W. Clement Stone. Og read it—and then walked all the way to Chicago to get a job with Stone's company, Combined Insurance, now the Aon Corporation.

Og's mother had always told him that one day he would be a great writer. He remembered what she said but did not see how it could ever happen to him. Og started doing some writing, which eventually found its way to the boss and the owner of both Combined Insurance and *Success Magazine*, Mr. Clem Stone himself. Stone read Og's words and said, "Wow, this is so good! You've got to write for us." Og wound up as editor in chief of *Success Magazine*. He loved to write and was so motivated to use it to help others that he wrote all of his books from 2:00 to 4:00 a.m. every morning, while his wife, family, and business concerns slept. He liked that time period because there were no phone calls, no family interruptions, or any other distractions.

During this time, Og wrote *The Greatest Salesman in the World*. It was published, and then Richard DeVoss, chairman of Amway read it, loved it, and featured it to all of his multitudes of representatives. The book wound up selling 38 million copies.

That's how it happened for a man from New Hampshire who was struggling with a drinking problem. He stopped drinking and changed his drinking addiction to an inspired writing addiction. Brilliant books emerged. How did his life begin to turn around? It was a connection with books. It started when he walked into that library and read Clem Stone's book. It continued when he began writing on his own. It accelerated into high gear when his book was published. Og ultimately got to live his passion: to write, travel, and speak full-time, wowing audiences everywhere. What his mother told him as a young boy was finally coming to fruition: he would someday be a great writer.

I have read and reread his inspiring books and encourage you to do the same. I recommend every one of Og's great books to everyone. I predict that you will become a lifelong fan.

Some of the bonuses of writing: you become a better reader, a more diligent follower of your favorite authors, a better conversationalist, a more accurate thinker, and more in demand as a wise friend.

Will it happen for you as it happened for Og Mandino? Probably not in every detail, but your own miracles will begin to happen, and I want to hear about them. Your commitment to writing a book—and your decision to read and use this one—are key first steps toward big-time success, both creatively and financially. So congratulations—and let's get started!

PART ONE

Write a GREAT Book!

Writing is simple and complicated, hard and easy, painful and pleasurable, natural and unnatural. It's a paradox—like so many other important things in life. There's a lot to say about writing from a philosophical standpoint, but philosophy isn't the focus of this book. I want to give you hands-on information and practical tools. I want to inspire you to find the book that's inside you (I know it's there!) and get it into the hands of thousands, even millions, of readers worldwide. You have something to say, and it is important that you say it. You know that, and that is why you are reading this book.

The first step is certainty. Not just confidence, not just belief, but the absolute *conviction* that you have a book inside you that is going to be born. It's the principle on which martial arts like karate are built. When you're punching your hand through a board, you don't focus on striking the wood itself. You concentrate on reaching though the wood to grasp something beyond it. Something you want. Something you need. Something you know is there.

You don't have to believe you can write. All you have to do now is believe that *I* believe you can write, and voilà: YOU REALLY CAN WRITE!

I give you permission and full encouragement to write. I want you to believe in yourself, in your writing ability, and in the phenomenal contribution that you will make to others. Repeat to yourself 101 times a night before you go to sleep: I AM A GREAT AND INSPIRING WRITER AND BEST-SELLING AUTHOR. Do this with feeling, belief, and total expectancy. Live in the assumption that your vision, purpose, and hope are fulfilled and that readers are loving, benefiting from, and automatically sharing your writings.

See yourself on the other side of the writing experience, just as a karate master sees his hand pass on to the other side of the board before he makes a move. That's why we will keep saying *live in your imagination, and start with the end in mind.* See your best seller in detail and all that it can mean to you, to your loved ones, and to the world. It costs no more to dream big and have high expectations for yourself. Do this faithfully every night for one month. By the month's end, you will have given yourself the autosuggestion that will make you a decisively great and inspiring writer and best-selling author. Soon you'll be thanking me in your nightly prayers.

When Jack Canfield and I were deep into the creation of *Chicken Soup for the Soul*, I had a proposed cover design from a graphic artist that I met in Canada. It cost us $1,500. It was worth every penny. We copied the cover and put it on the mirrors in my home and office bathrooms, and in Jack's.

As I will relate in future pages in depth, I interviewed 101 of the world's best-selling fiction and nonfiction authors, not on how to write, but on how they effectively and successfully marketed their best sellers. From their wisdom, insights, ideas, and how-tos, I wrote what we called a WOW OF A BOOK BUSINESS PLAN, aimed at selling a million and a half books in a year and a half.

Most importantly, we were visually impregnating the end result of becoming *New York Times* best-selling authors in our minds as a completed task. Dr. M. Scott Peck, a colleague of Jack's from Harvard, had been at number one for fifty-eight weeks in a row, with the superlatively important *A Road Less Traveled.* We copied his number one book placement, whited out his name, inserted ours, and placed it on top of our new book cover. Thus every time we, our family, or staff went into the bathroom, we were impressing on our minds the future truth that we planned to express: that we were number one bestsellers like our colleague and friend Dr. Peck. We were teased, hassled, and harassed about our bodacious behavior, but the result is worth the criticism. No one remembered their criticism of us after we accomplished what seemed ridiculous and impossible to those who were ignorant of the "visualizing is realizing" principle. I even made an entire set of audios that are still available, called *Visualizing Is Realizing*. It's a must-do principle that works effectively in all areas of your life.

Before you read any further, please take a little time to contemplate what you're about to do. Again, since we're going to be focusing on the tools of writing, I will toss in pertinent philosophical ideas that will help you set your internal GPS and give you the strength to continue despite the odds. These tools work best when the motivation and the commitment are already solidly in place.

Your inner resilience will come from your nightly 101 repetitions of the mantra above. That autosuggestion will help you commit to write faithfully *every day* until your work is complete, finished, published, and selling in massive numbers.

Once you really have the confidence that defines all successful writers, here's something about which I am certain: the information contained in these pages is the best resource anywhere for building your career as a writer. As a writer myself, I've wanted to publish this book for a long time. It contains *everything* I've learned about all aspects of writing, from the blank page to the shelves of Barnes & Noble and to Amazon.com worldwide sales.

I respect and admire this exciting path of authorship that you have chosen, because it's the same thing I wanted for myself. With all humility, I'm proud to say I love writing, reading, and thinking about the entire process. Even with as much success as I have had as an author, I continue to write more books to this day. I love doing it, and I don't ever want to stop. I believe my best books, audios, videos, podcasts, plays, and movies are yet to be created. I think I am writing better than ever and am enjoying the experience more than ever.

Trust me: you can do it too. Starting right now.

The First Absolute Essential: Your Basic Message

What are the *absolute essentials* for a powerful and successful nonfiction book? As it happens, there are four of them. If you learn nothing else from this book, I urge you to take these four absolute essentials to heart.

First, your book must have an *interesting and important message* to convey. At first, this might seem obvious, but an amazing number of writers fail to clearly define their message. What message do you want to move from your head into the hearts of your readers?

For example: Is global climate change risking our survival as a species and something we need to deal with right now? Or is global climate change a hyped-up myth? In terms of getting your book organized and written, it doesn't really matter what you think is the truth. What matters is that *you* are utterly convinced that you know the truth, that you understand it and can prove it, and that you urgently need to share it with your readers. As we all know, former vice president Al Gore believed his message about global warming. He wrote about it, created a seminar on it, and made *An Inconvenient Truth*, a movie based on his message. Gore's passion for his message rang so true that he won an Academy Award and a Nobel Peace Prize and donated over $300 million of his earnings to help end global warming. If you haven't seen this important work, rent it and watch it. Use this as an example to see how far passion combined with excellent writing can take you.

The Second Absolute Essential: Stories about Other People

Your life, my life, and everyone's life are stories. Telling better stories means you will have a better life. Stories are more than a luxury, more than just entertainment. Human beings have always relied upon stories to process their lives, their relationships, their past, and their future. Since the beginning of time, every society has provided ways for people to connect through narratives about other peoples' lives. In ancient times there were ritual storytellers and dramas. This oral tradition—telling stories around the campfire—was how people passed on culture, history, tradition, and morals. Today there are films, books, plays, and other media, but the need to find out about other human beings will endure forever.

Don't miss *any* opportunity for storytelling in your book. Whenever you make a major point about your message, illustrate it with a brief anecdote or a fully developed narrative. Whether this requires only one paragraph or several pages, the purpose is to *show* your readers what you're talking about, not just *tell* them. In professional speaking, we teach the same process: make a point and tell a story. Stories are heard, remembered, and repeated.

The Third Absolute Essential: Stories about You

When you read a book, a genuinely intimate connection is formed between you and the writer. Or more accurately, it's the writer's job to see that such a connection develops. By the end of the book, the reader should know you as more than combinations of letters on a page. If you do your job well, you can really come alive for your audience in a mysterious, magical, memorable, and almost mystical way. You will live as a person in the reader's mind.

This has to be done carefully, however. It's not just a matter of pasting your bio or résumé onto the page. The reader should learn about you over the course of the entire book—a little here and a little there. It all adds up to knowing you through the experiences you share, respecting you, and (most importantly) *liking* you.

Look at the advertisements that major publishers run in book reviews for their new releases. What do you notice about the pictures of the authors in the ads? They look like people you'd want to hang out with—people with whom it would be fun to share a meal or a beer. What you feel when you look at those pictures is *exactly* what you want your readers to feel as they read your book.

The Fourth Absolute Essential: Action Steps for the Reader

The word *takeaway* should be in the forefront of every writer's mind. What do you want your readers to take with them and use in their everyday lives after they've read your book? You want to cause instant behavioral change.

One great example is from my friend Jeff Hoffman, serial entrepreneur, author, filmmaker, Grammy Award

Winner, software engineer, billionaire, best known as creator of Priceline and the kiosks that enable you to print your ticket for your airline seat. Jeff is a master storyteller and a relatable thinker. He inspires everyone to believe that they can create a fortune and have a fulfilling and enjoyable life doing it. Please watch him online. Jeff teaches what he calls the Golden Purpose. It is the intersection of (1) the work you are best at; (2) the thing you love, and (3) what the world values enough to pay you substantially to do. With regard to number one, Jeff advises you to ask ten friends to write out and submit to you what each of them thinks you are best at doing. He says you will be pleasantly surprised and delighted. Asking ten friends is a specific takeaway that can instantly change your behavior.

If you do your job correctly, readers will gain a lot more than some abstract ideas. They'll take away information you've provided, things that they can use in their own lives, steps they can take right now to put what they've learned into action.

This is a critically important component of a book—and one that's often overlooked by writers. The day is long gone when people read books simply for entertainment. Today people buy nonfiction books the same way they buy over-the-counter medicines. *They want results!* They're willing to work for those results, provided they're told (by you) exactly what that work should involve.

Providing action steps for your readers to follow are the fourth and final absolute essential for your book. Put that step into action!

The One Question Every Writer Must Answer

You've got a story to tell. You've got valuable information to share. I hope what you've read so far has assured you of that. I hope you also understand that many people—including you—will benefit when you tell your story and share your wisdom.

So what's the first step? That's a really important question, because the first step in writing a book is really the most challenging.

Again and again I've seen new writers sitting at a keyboard with a blank screen in front of them. Or if the screen isn't totally blank, it's a battleground of revisions and corrections that add up to nothing much.

The cause of all, this, of course, is the writer's belief that the first sentence has to be "perfect"—and not just the first sentence, but the book as a whole. After all, this isn't just a letter to Grandma we're writing here. This is a book that's going to be sold in stores, just like the complete works of Shakespeare, not to mention the Bible. We're going to ask people to pay good money for this, so it has to be great. It has to be clean and shiny and fussed over, just like the seventh-grade term papers you nervously wrote and carefully stored in a transparent plastic binder.

Your book has to be perfect, doesn't it?

No, it doesn't. In fact, you shouldn't even try for perfection—because if you do, you're much more likely to get nothing at all. With this in mind, I'm now going to reveal the one question you should always be asking yourself in order to avoid perfectionism and get what's in your mind onto the paper in front of you.

The question is, *What are you trying to say?* To show you exactly why that seemingly innocent question is so powerful and important, let me dramatize it for you.

Picture sitting at your computer, contemplating what you're going to write. Or imagine you're revising—for the fifth time—what you've written so far. At that moment, your best friend calls, and before long, the conversation turns to the trouble you're having with your book.

"I just can't seem to get it right," you explain. "I know what I want to get on the page, but I can't find the correct words for saying it."

At that point your friend asks a logical question: "What are you trying to say?" So you explain what you're trying to say—and then, when the phone conversation is over, you're back to *trying* to say it.

But what if, when your friend asked, "What are you trying to say?" you had just gone ahead and written down your answer? What if you just stopped trying and started writing? It's amazing how simple this is. I've seen it work again and again with writers who seem to be hopelessly bogged down. Ask yourself—or imagine that a close friend is asking—"What are you trying to say?"

Then immediately write down your answer, word for word. Don't think about it. Just write it, and then use your momentum to continue writing. If you get stuck, ask the magic question again. If you're not entirely happy with what's on the page, you can go back over it later or—that's what editors are for. But now you're moving ahead. On the first pass you may not get everything exactly right, but you will get it *written*.

You have unique knowledge to communicate. You have information that no one else has. So don't feel you have to morph into someone else—not Mark Victor Hansen, not even William Shakespeare—when you actually start typing. You can avoid that temptation by continually asking, "What am I trying to say?" and simply writing your answer to that question on the page. It should be on the page exactly as you express it in your own mind, rather than the way you think anyone else would say it.

Get Used to It!

Writing is a challenging, complicated activity—and virtually all activities of this kind are hard the first time you try them. Writing can be painful—mentally, emotionally, and even physically. It can also be hugely rewarding and exhilarating. But you've got to get used to it. You've got to get over that panic and stop feeling like it's the first day of school or your first date.

Even for the most successful writers, filling up the page isn't always easy. Joyce Carol Oates is one of the most acclaimed fiction writers of our time. She's written approximately sixty novels, plus short stories, poetry, nonfiction, and even children's books.

In a National Book Award interview, Oates said, "Each day is like an enormous rock that I'm trying to push up this hill. I get it up a fair distance, it rolls back a little bit, and I keep pushing it, hoping I'll get it to the top of the hill and that it will go on its own momentum. But I've never given up. I've always kept going. I don't feel that I could afford to give up. Yet I am not conscious of working especially hard, or of 'working' at all. Writing and teaching have always been, for me, so richly rewarding that I don't think of them as work in the usual sense of the word."

Simply put, Oates is used to the process of putting words on the page. It may not always be easy, but it's natural. That's the way it is for professional writers. It can't be something you do only once in a while. You've got to write as much as you can! You've got to feel at home with it. Writing has to become a natural action that you do all the time.

This is an area where I feel I've made some real progress. I try to write for at least a couple of hours every day. Airplanes are an especially good writing workplace. The airplane is my office in the sky. Talking is a big part of my life, but I don't talk on planes. I just keep working, and people leave me alone. I'm not there to impress anyone. I'm trying to get from one place to another, both in the sky and on the page.

Early in my career as a speaker and writer, I traveled a bit with America's most beloved minister, Dr. Norman Vincent Peale, author of the must-read book that has sold 25 million copies: *The Power of Positive Thinking*. This was before computers. Dr. Peale carried two big briefcases filled with folders for his fifty-two future church sermons at New York's prestigious Marble Collegiate Church and for books and pamphlets that he intended to write.

Dr. Peale told me that once he titled the fifty-two sermon files—which he did before the start of each year started—the information seemed to magically and mystically flow to and through him. It is the law of attraction in action. He had the attractor factor working, and so can you. People would say things innocently, and he would record what they told him. Dr. Peale stashed their stories in his files for future use. He created a mindset that would attract stories, anecdotes, jokes, humor, experiences, and memories that would make his sermons awe-inspiring, dynamic, and wonderfully insightful.

While living in New York, I went to Dr. Peale's church faithfully every Sunday and met the who's who of the world. Mrs. Peale took a liking to me. She frequently invited me to sit with her and the corporate, business, and world leaders who were attending, in awe of Dr. Peale's relatable and repeatable wisdom.

I was at Dr. Peale's church one Sunday when President Richard Nixon and his family were sitting happily in the balcony. Everyone knew they were there. Whispers and upward glances cascaded through America's first megachurch.

When it came time to pray, Dr. Peale had all of us close our eyes, fold our hands, bow our heads, and pray. When he finished, he said, "We are all delighted to have the esteemed president and his family here with us at Marble Collegiate Church today. And I know all his bodyguards and Secret Service agents who are in attendance, because when I told you to close your eyes, I kept mine open. It is him, him, him, and him." The audience roared with laughter. The president laughed, smiled, stood, waved, thankful for the titter that went through the crowd. That's why Dr. Peale's stories were so captivating: they were real, relevant, compelling, and fun, with unique and unexpected surprises.

The bonus point I am making is that you are to have a self-actualizing life that is unlimited, enchanting, and exciting to live, have, and write about. It is not just for

Ernest Hemingway, Dr, Wayne Dyer, Ian Fleming, or Diana Gabaldon to have a wow of a life. It's for you, me, and everyone. Life is not a dress rehearsal. We can't wait to retire to try new exciting things.

Bob Allen, my coauthor of three books starting with *The One Minute Millionaire*, called and asked if I would go to open the pyramids in Guatemala and help write about it with the head of archeology and anthropology at Harvard, Dr. Bill Saturno. I jumped at the chance. I thought that it would provide a lot of great stories to tell, and it did. Every author who works his or her craft with excellence will be invited to write stories about experiences that are ordinarily unimaginable, but they are coming and you will have them.

Likewise, I have the titles of over two hundred books, audio, and podcasts that I want to write. My computer is loaded with great ideas and concepts that I want to work on and with. Even as I write this, on a plane en route to Warren Buffett's annual Berkshire Hathaway extravaganza, thoughts flood my mind. I quickly switch on the computer screen and instantly capture great ideas that I will use in the future. Hopefully, you will do the same or even better with all of your ideas. Also, perhaps you will become one of my raving fans and read more of what I write. I am an enormous fan of many writers, have read everything written by many of the greats, and plan to do so for as long as I live. Maybe that sounds like you too.

Being a habitual writer doesn't mean you have to be working on your book, or books, all the time. A great way to feel at home with writing is by sending letters to your friends. An actual, physical letter can have a big impact. (Remember to keep copies of your correspondences and archive them. You, your heirs, your biographer, and your archivist will be glad you did.)

Steve Gottry and I have just finished a new series of Speed Write books. It behooves me especially to share one title that I hope you will get. Called *Speed Write Your Life Story or Autobiography*, it will, as its title suggests, enable you to write your life story. We recommend that you write it in ninety days by writing twenty-two minutes per day. Wouldn't it be nice if your great-great-great-grandparents had done that so you knew your ancestral history and their experiences in times gone by?

Texting, video recordings, email, and instant messages have made letter writing almost a lost art. But many of our finest authors were fanatical letter writers, sending handwritten correspondence back and forth on a scale that seems almost unimaginable today. Even Abraham Lincoln, Albert, Einstein, Ronald Reagan, and Mahatma Gandhi found time to write thousands of letters.

So, yes, learning to write requires *writing*—and by the way, it also requires *reading*. Oddly, many aspiring writers read very little, or they only read one kind of material.

Don't expect to find millions of readers for your book if you don't read widely yourself.

A Writing Secret from "Raging Bill" Shakespeare

In *Macbeth*, Bill Shakespeare wrote, "If it were done, 'tis best it were done quickly." Bill was referring to murder, but he could just as well have meant writing a book. Writers must learn to write fast and intuitively. I suggest you write out everything you can think of in your own natural style before you study a subject in depth. Write out your original thinking first, and then do your research. It will help you in every way to create, complete, and realize your own thoughts.

In my writing and businesses, I offer three keys: (1) be original, (2) be transformational, and (3) be inevitable. Chicken Soup was the original series of heart-touching and soul-penetrating stories that transformed readers, and inevitably they had what the literary industry calls pass-along value. The pass-along value of our readership in America is five: each of our books is passed along to five other readers. During the two weeks when Jack Canfield talked, toured, and lectured in India, he was on the covers of their equivalents of *Time*, *Sports Illustrated*, and *Forbes* in the two weeks' time. He was told that books there are so rare and expensive that pass-along value was over fifteen readers per book. Jack brought back a giant three-ring binder of press clippings about his monumentally heroic reception in India. It was a wow to behold.

In China, I have been told, each of our books is read by twelve readers, it has been reported to me. My wife, Crystal, and I have had enormous, positive, exciting, and memorable receptions throughout China. Our phenomenal promoter and lifelong friend, Dr. David Chu, had our Mark and Crystal Hansen Foundation and the Giant Bicycle Company Foundation give bicycles for a number of Chinese orphans to ride next to the Great Wall of China. The media loved it and monitored and broadcast it widely. Families who either couldn't have children or wanted to and could afford more children adopted these orphans. We got to meet many of the children that were lovingly adopted. We met the chairman and CEO of Giant Bicycle Company, and we rode bicycles with them through one of the famed Chinese cities.

Another approach is taken by friend and colleague Brian Tracy, the man I call the encyclopedia of our speaking and writing business. The prolific Isaac Asimov wrote over five hundred books and an estimated 90,000 letters and postcards. I expect my friend will eclipse his giant body of work.

As an adult Brian has mastered German and Spanish and created programs in these languages as well. Brian reads fifty great books on a subject of interest, makes himself an expert, and puts his material together as an audio program. Later he goes back and turns it into a book—at a rate of four published books per year. He's covered over three hundred separate topics.

The point is this: there are countless ways to get your ideas into print. Throughout the book, I will give you several options. If you have one that you think I missed or should consider, please send me a note; my address is at the front (and back) of this book. I see this book as an evolving work in progress. I want your help to constantly and continuously improve it for all future readers.

Nevertheless, constant reworking of a manuscript can have a deadening effect. It happens all the time: proposals and even complete books go stale as a result of excessive polishing.

The worst enemy you face as a writer is the blank page. It's as simple as that. In order to beat this enemy, you need (at least in the beginning) to value speed over accuracy in your writing. As someone once said, "Beginning authors focus on getting it right. Experienced authors focus on getting it written." As the late inspirational speaker and pastor Dr. Robert Schuller Sr. said, "Begun is half done."

Obviously there are limits on how far you can take this principle. Unless you're a rare genius, your work will need to be revised and edited, perhaps more than once. You can deal with that later. The first task is to do *something*. If it's something wrong, at least it is something. Again, you can fix it later. The industrialist, writer, and philanthropist Peter J. Daniels, author of *How to Be Happy though Rich* told me: "You can fix something; you can't fix nothing."

There is one caveat to this principle. You must have at least a minimal knowledge of grammar and correct English usage. This is something that can't be taken for granted today, since many schools no longer teach "readin'-'n'-writin'" as they used to. If you're unsure about your grammatical skills, go online. There are loads of websites that can help you. Once you've mastered the basics, you can start putting them into action without making a huge number of mistakes that will have to be corrected later on. Learning grammar fundamentals is really a small price to pay for success in the writing business. You may have the mental equivalent of a Ferrari in your mind and heart, but you'll still have to pass the test for a driver's license.

A Writing Secret from Wayne Newton

In some years, entertainer Wayne Newton did two shows a night, 365 nights a year, in Las Vegas.

When you're onstage that much, lots of challenges arise. Just the physical strength that's required is amazing! But the biggest challenge, as he explained in a *60 Minutes* interview, was finding a way to make *every* show seem special. You've got an audience of people who are seeing you for their first, and probably only, time. How can you give them the feeling that this is as exciting for you as it is for them when you've already done this same show on 10,000 prior occasions?

The solution is simple, but not necessarily easy—and it's very pertinent to what's involved in being an effective writer.

You certainly need to communicate your understanding of the readers' needs, but you must also convey your *own* excitement in creating the book. You've got to feel that excitement yourself before you can share it. When I was speaking in Australia, a lady named Natasha told me that my new book *Cash in a Flash* emotionally jumped off the page as she read it and inspired her to become a successful entrepreneur. That happened to her as a reader because I felt it as a writer.

Writing can be hard and sometimes tedious work, but even as you're slogging through it, you need to experience it as the most exhilarating thing in the world. Until you're thrilled yourself, don't expect to thrill anybody else. Spiritual teacher Ram Dass, formerly Dr. Richard Alpert, once told me that every author should be mandated to write on the back cover of their book their prevailing attitude while composing it. Was it positive or negative?

Every writer must find his or her own way to get primed for the task. I can tell you this: if you're feeling really bogged down—not just lazy, but genuinely out of gas—it's time to take a break. Anything you write while you're in that state of mind will have to be redone later, so you're better off not doing it in the first place. Go back to your project when you're able to connect with a higher level of energy.

When Jack Canfield and I wrote *Chicken Soup for the Soul* along with our other collaborations, it was our practice to write for two hours and then walk together around the neighborhood, discussing our dreams for the book. Our dream walk and talks fueled us to manifest a system that has now generated over two hundred fifty-four books, and we are over 50 percent of the way to achieving our giant dream of selling over 1 billion books. We kindled our passion to be unstoppable in our desires and activities. We were thinking out loud about the system we were creating in order to make it everything it has become.

A Writing Secret from Michael Crichton

The late Michael Crichton was one of the most commercially successful writers of the twentieth century. In addition to his many novels, he created the Jurassic Park films and the *ER* television series. Crichton, a licensed MD trained at Harvard Medical School, had an amazing ability to explain and dramatize complex scientific concepts in a simple and easy to understand way. That is true genius. How did he do it?

The secret was to always go from a specific incident to a general principle—the inductive method. Crichton started putting this approach to work in one of his first books, entitled *Five Patients.* Instead of making grand pronouncements about health and healing, he told the stories of five flesh-and-blood human beings. The principles emerged from the stories, rather than the other way around. (Deductive writing and thinking can also work. My great and inspiring teacher, Dr. R. Buckminster Fuller, wrote forty books, starting deductively from the universe to specifics. Each form can be effectively utilized.)

Readers don't like to be preached at. Even in a nonfiction book, they want to read *stories.* So one of your most important tasks is finding the story that most effectively communicates your concept. The way to do this isn't always obvious, and it isn't always easy. But no matter what your topic is, the human story is always there. The phenomenon of climate change expresses itself in one person's air conditioning bill. Fluctuations in gas prices mean rescheduled family vacations. Start small, and then widen the focus. That's the rule.

A Writing Secret from Mario Puzo

If you don't want your book to sleep with the fishes, the author of *The Godfather* had some good advice. Mario

Puzo never showed his work to anyone until he felt that he was really done with it. He resisted the temptation to get feedback because he saw it for what it was: a desire to receive congratulations for having written a book before it was actually written. Of course, negative feedback could be even more dangerous. Writers can be so devastated by criticism at an early stage of a book's development that they give up on the project altogether. That's like being depressed because your child hasn't gotten into Harvard—even though your child hasn't been born yet.

Although Puzo was against showing a work in progress to anyone, there might be a couple of exceptions to this rule. For example, there can be benefits to getting feedback from a carefully selected reader whom you don't know too well, but for whom you have real respect. Because of the distance in your relationship, your emotional response to what you learn can be manageable.

You can get good information—and inspiration too—from joining a writing group. Somehow sharing your work in a group setting has a different effect than an individual exchange.

In short: be aware of the potential impact of showing an unfinished work. Keep in mind the saying, "Never show a fool a job half done." Within certain limits, you may still want to share your work in progress. Just not with fools. Or with really close friends.

A Writing Secret from Jimmy Breslin

The late Jimmy Breslin may have been the last of what were once called *newspapermen.* That is, someone who takes taxis around a big city at all hours of the night and is known to every driver, who hangs out with off-duty detectives in smoke-filled bars, and who manages to make every deadline for his daily column, if only at the last minute.

That's Jimmy Breslin, who for many years was a columnist in New York and was the author of several interesting novels and at least one biography. Sometimes Breslin would give advice to others who, like him, had chosen the writing profession. Although his first piece of advice ("Ask for more money") doesn't deal with the process of writing itself, Breslin also came up with an extremely useful insight for writing well.

It's actually very simple. When you've written a sentence, pause for a second and challenge yourself to take one word out of the sentence without changing the meaning. You may find that it doesn't actually improve when you do this, in which case you can just leave it as it was. But almost always the sentence will improve—and the time it takes to do the "extraction" will translate into time saved later on, when your book is in the editing process.

A Writing Secret from Neil Simon

Surprising as it may seem, great works of art like Michelangelo's *Pietà* weren't created simply by emotion and inspiration. From the days of ancient Greece and Rome through the Renaissance, artists of all kinds used carefully worked out mathematical formulas as the foundation for their highly emotional or even spiritual creations.

This was also true of poets and dramatists. In fact, the most successful writers still take a very rational approach to their work, (although the trick is to keep this fact well-hidden). Neil Simon, for example, who created *The Odd Couple* and dozens of other hugely successful comedies for stage and screen, is known for carefully following the Rule of Three. Wikipedia describes it as follows:

> The Rule of Three is a principle in English writing that suggests that things that come in threes are inherently funnier, more satisfying, or more effective than other numbers of things. A series of three is often used to create a progression in which the tension is created, then built up, and finally released. From slogans ("Go, fight, win!") to films, many things are structured in threes: There were three musketeers, three little pigs, Goldilocks and the three bears, and Three Stooges.

When you're looking for the most effective way to write about an idea or incident, keep the Rule of Three in mind. First, the concept is introduced, then repeated and intensified, and finally concluded at some later point. This principle can be used over the course of an entire book, in an individual chapter, or even in a single paragraph.

The Rule of Three will prevent you from winging it in your writing. The greatest writers never wing it, even though that's exactly what they seem to be doing.

A Writing Secret from George Orwell

George Orwell, the author of *1984*, was a great champion of individual freedom. Consequently, he hated any form of restriction or forced restraint, especially pertaining to thought and language. For this reason, Orwell was very sensitive about clichés. He saw them as thinly disguised barriers to genuine self-expression and self-realization.

In guidelines for fellow writers, Orwell was very clear on this point: never use a figure of speech that you've previously seen in print. Certainly this is good advice, but it's not always easy to follow. Stock phrases are everywhere in the media, and they creep into the way we express ourselves in all sorts of situations, including the writing of books. In fact, many readers actually appreciate a writer who uses prepackaged phrases and ideas. That doesn't necessarily mean you should do it—Orwell would be horrified—but the issue is a little more complicated than it might seem.

As a commercially oriented writer, your first job is to connect with the widest possible audience. That connection begins with your readers' sense that you're one of them. Complete originality of thought and expression is something to be prized in writing based on complete self-expression. But when writing is your business, you've got to meet your customers—that is, your readers—where they are. At the end of the day (there's a stock phrase!), using the language that you hear every day can be an effective tool for connecting with everyday people. Just make it a choice, not a reflex.

A Writing Secret from Stephen King

As a writer, you must learn discipline. At the same time, you have to learn the difference between discipline and drudgery. How can you make the act of writing enjoyable, so that you *want* to do it every day? What's the difference between procrastination and creative time wasting?

Stephen King has described writing as "a great way to pass the time." That may sound like a humorous comment from someone who has probably sold more books than anybody else alive. But I think he really meant it. King spoke of how he would write late at night while listening to Bruce Springsteen songs cranked up to a high volume. Honestly, I think there's nowhere else Stephen King would rather have been.

In the same spirit, Mario Puzo used to lie on his back on a sofa, staring up at the ceiling. That could go on for a long time. Once his wife got up the nerve to ask him what he was doing. Without taking his eyes off the ceiling, Puzo replied, "I'm working." And he meant it.

That's the thing about being a writer. To other people, it may look like you're wasting time. Sometimes you really *are* wasting time. Only you know the difference.

You Need a Great Title

Be careful not to become too invested in the first title you think of for your book. You need a great title—something that's going to make the reader's heart positively *sing*! With your title, you're asking your potential buyers, "Will you give me $20 for this book?" If the answer to your title's question is no, then it's not the title you need.

Titles are everything! They're the door to the house. They invite you in or keep you out. Decide to be a masterful, confident, competent title writer for yourself and others. Writers always talk to other writers, so get into the habit of thinking, eating, breathing, living, and talking titles. You will create an amazing amount of superstar titles.

Keep a file of titles. Keep adding to them. As your name, fame, and reputation expand and grow, you will be spontaneously asked to write more. Editors, agents, publishers, and companies will ask, "What have you got for a title?" and you will say, "This, this, and this!" Set a goal for yourself of writing at least one title each and every day for the rest of your life. Soon you will have a feel for what will sell and become a hand-along book. That's industry jargon for a book that everyone promotes, like *The Da Vinci Code* by Dan Brown, which has sold over 50 million copies and has been made into a Ron Howard film. Soon you will be able to tell when you have a title destined to become a big, best-selling winner.

Rodale Press sends out direct mail pieces with twenty different titles of upcoming books to their target market. They send the book to all buyers with a note that essentially says: "This is the book you ordered, and we hope you are happy with it. The marketplace suggested to us that this is the preferred title." They go with whatever title has the most traction.

Jack Canfield and I began our Chicken Soup project with several working titles. In fact, one night we sat in my Jacuzzi and wrote 139 titles that we wanted to write someday—but no title matched the product and system that we had zealously created.

We ultimately tried a process that had been used by Napoleon Hill to come up with *Think and Grow Rich*: You close your eyes, and behind your closed eyelids, you tip your eyes up at a forty-five-degree angle. Then you say,

"Mega-best-selling title, mega-best-selling title, mega-best-selling title." You should do this four hundred times in a row just before going to sleep. Give yourself a thought command telling you that you will wake up at a predetermined time, say 4 a.m., with your title. It worked for us, it worked for Dr. Hill, and it can work for you.

When doing this, remember to have pen and paper or a recording device next to the bed. Why? The famous comedian Red Skelton told me that he had a complete vision for a play in the middle of the night and was certain that he wrote it down. When he woke in the morning, he could not remember anything from the play—the story, the plotline, or even a word—but he knew it was brilliant. He looked at his notepad and, to his utter and absolute dismay, it said, "Write play."

A title is the open sesame to a great best seller. It takes only a little time and effort to indulge in this process, and the payoff can be enormous.

On the night we agreed to do our autosuggestion programming, Jack woke at 4:00 a.m. with the title *Chicken Soup for the Soul.* He called me and woke up my then wife. She said, "This had better be good." Well, it *was* good. That's how the title came about. You might want to try the thought command method for yourself, or any other means you can think of. But no matter what, you've got to have a great title.

Jillian Manus, my phenomenal literary agent, suggests having a title party. Invite your wisest and smartest friends over for a barbecue, wine, and great thinking. Tell them in advance that they have been selected to help you create extraordinary best-selling titles that you will be writing into history. Great friends love to help, inspire, and contribute to your ever greater successes.

Build Up Your Life outside of Your Work

Regardless of its topic, your book is who you are. If you're doing nothing, being nothing, and having nothing in your life, why would anyone want to read your book?

Don't expect your book to be your life. Have a life before you write your book. Otherwise a desperate quality will creep into your writing, and that's something you don't want. Personally, I became a mountain climber four years ago and have climbed, or climbed on, Mount Whitney, Mount Kilimanjaro, Mount Fuji, and Machu Picchu. I promise this makes for great storytelling, and I will include these stories in my forthcoming autobiography, entitled *Mark on Mark!*

Remember that you need a great title. What is its real function? Remember that the title is the door to the home called your book. Doors provide easy access to a home: no one except a thief wants to come in through the window.

Make the door easy, friendly, inviting, and compelling so that the reader desperately wants to enter your story. For the reader, it opens the door to your world. So there has to be somethingin that world of yours that the reader really wants to know about and take part in.

Print Out Your Work and Read It Aloud

You can't get in touch with what you've put on the page just by reading your work on your computer screen. After all, a computer screen is not a page! So you've got to print out a hard copy in order to see what's really there.

That's not the end, however. You should also read your words aloud, preferably to someone you know and trust—but not too well. By reading your work aloud to a comparative stranger, you'll really notice what's working and what's not. You'll get puzzled looks from your audience at things that seemed perfectly clear to you when you wrote them. You'll also get a positive response from passages that you weren't sure about. The one thing you don't want is the kind of blanket praise that you're likely to get from a very close friend. So be careful in choosing your listener.

The master of this process is Jim Trelease, who talks to hundreds of thousands of people annually about his book *Read Aloud*. Jim says the best thing you can do for children and adults alike to improve their relationships, thinking, and future is to read aloud to them daily. I hired Jim to talk several times when my kids were in elementary school, because I thought his messages were profound and absolutely right on.

Read your stories out loud to interested individuals. Jack and I tested all our stories on lots of people. When we found a story we thought would really connect with a friend of ours, we immediately called him or her and shared the story. Their acceptance, insights, and statements helped our Chicken Soup series become a spectacular success.

Get Used to the Editorial Process

Almost all writers find it very difficult to go over their own work objectively. The amount of time and energy needed to create a finished document makes the possibility of more time and effort hugely unappetizing. But if you intend to be a published author, you've got to get used to the editorial process.

Winston Churchill edited his works fourteen times before sharing them, even with his editor. Ernest Hemingway said, "Write drunk and edit sober." I think that means be intoxicated, excited, and enchanted by your writing, and look at your editing process through several sets of eyes: the eyes of an editor, reader, disinterested third party, and book buyer.

Sooner or later, your work is going to be critiqued by someone—hopefully by the editor who's given you a contract. It's in your best interest to have your book in solid shape as soon as possible. Creating a hard copy and reading it out loud are essential steps.

If You Don't Write, Don't Do Anything Else!

Raymond Chandler was a trailblazing novelist and screenwriter from the 1930s through the 1950s. Along with a few other writers, he essentially created the modern detective story and the hard-boiled private eye.

As it happens, Chandler also had a neurotic personality and found it difficult to complete a project, or even to start one. He was always looking for the magic bullet that would cure his writer's block. At one point, he was sure he'd found the answer. When he sat down at his desk, he gave himself permission not to write if he really couldn't think of anything. But he also denied himself permission to do anything else: no newspapers, no phone calls—just the blank wall behind the typewriter. Chandler's theory was that the sensory deprivation would become so unpleasant that he'd eventually start writing in spite of himself.

Did it work? Not exactly as he'd hoped, but the principle is interesting. Some writers are hard-core procrastinators. These people really will turn even a slight distraction into a daylong avoidance mechanism. If that's your situation, you really should eliminate every possible time waster in order to get something done.

Other writers are actually more productive when a certain number of distractions are available. You've got to figure this one out for yourself from your personal writing style. You may need to waste some time now and then in order to use the rest of your time effectively. So go ahead: read the paper, or play an online game. On the other hand, you may need to go cold turkey and eliminate every other possibility except for one—actually writing.

Danielle Steele, one of the most commercially successful writers of all time, has 179 published novels and has sold over 800 million books. She also has seven children, and to avoid distraction she spends hours locked in a closet in order to write. She owns one of the biggest homes in the prestigious Pacific Heights district of San Francisco. Standing at the park above her home and looking down at her estate, one can really appreciate its enormity. Now picture her writing all those best-selling books and screenplays hiding in a tiny closet to avoid interruptions and distractions. If you have to go this route, just make sure there's an adequate air supply!

Note: there are infinite systems, ways, and processes to make your book happen. I am showing you a smorgasbord of models to help you feel comfortable with one that can make you insanely successful.

Keep Paragraphs Short

Ernest Hemingway said that writing was easy; it only became difficult if you expected somebody else to read what you wrote. That's what we're learning to do here: write so that not only somebody will read it, but will *want* to read it and want to *keep on reading.*

To keep your readers reading, limit chapters to ten pages or less. That's the length even the most attentive readers can absorb before they go to sleep at night, wait on the plane at takeoff or landing, sit in the bathroom, or avoid the work they have to do on their computer.

As much as possible, start the sentences with action-oriented verbs. The master of this is Dan Brown in *The Da Vinci Code.* I have read all of Dan's books, and no one puts more action into a sentence, paragraph, or an entire book than Dan does.

It's amazing how following a few simple rules can help you keep your readers reading. For instance, market research has shown that consumers respond much better to ad copy when the paragraphs contain no more than eight lines. It doesn't really matter how long the whole ad is. In fact, longer ads are usually better. (The best long form copywriter is Jay Abraham, my great friend and the man with whom I share the same birth date as Elvis Presley.) But within the document, the paragraphs must conform to the eight-line limit.

What works in advertising may be irrelevant to your writing—unless, as Hemingway said, you actually expect someone to read it! If you really get on a roll, you may find that you can fill page after page with long paragraphs or even solid text. That's a great feeling, and you should definitely roll with it. But afterwards, edit your work so that there are five or eight short paragraphs on each page, not two or three long ones. That will keep your readers happy! But don't take my word for it. The next time you're in a bookstore, pick up some best-selling books and check out the lengths of the paragraphs. (Uh-oh! This paragraph is getting *much* too long!)

Use Dialogue as Much as Possible

I'm looking at random through my copy of *The Da Vinci Code*. What I see resembles a play as much as a novel. The large amount of dialogue really opens up the page, so that readers aren't faced with a dense onslaught of text. It captures you in a conversation that you continue having in your mind.

Face it: we live in an age when people aren't really used to reading books, and they're getting less comfortable with it all the time. So make it easy for them. Even in a nonfiction book, dramatize your ideas by expressing them through conversations between recognizable human beings. Be creative about it. Don't say there's no way to use dialogue in a book about investment banking. Just have somebody yelling, "Help!"

A word of caution: you shouldn't portray imaginary conversations as if they really happened. Using condensed or edited versions of actual conversations is fine; just be clear about the fact that you're using hypothetical characters. When your book becomes an international sensation, there's a slight chance that someone will ask you to verify what you've written. It should be verifiable, or it should be so obviously unverifiable that nobody will ask the question in the first place.

Work on More than One Project at a Time

Before there was Jimmy Fallon, there was Johnny Carson, and before Johnny Carson, there was Steve Allen. This was the man who invented the television talk show, whose form has remained unchanged for more than fifty years.

This was a notable achievement, but no more so than Steve's accomplishments as a writer. He wrote more than 8,000 songs—hits like "This Could Be the Start of Something Big," as well as poems, plays, magazine articles, and fifty-four published books.

Obviously this was not a guy who had a problem getting words onto the page. Or was he? The truth is, Steve Allen was dyslexic and read backwards and upside down.

So he hit many walls, just like any other writer. But unlike other writers, he responded to stalling out on one project by getting to work on another project. He always had several going at the same time.

Steve told me that he had twenty-eight tape recorders, each linked to a different project. Steve said he might have writer's block on one project, so would stop on that one and go to work on another. "I have never had writer's block on twenty-eight projects simultaneously," he said. Eventually he finished them all.

Steve Allen generously came to our West Hollywood signing of *Chicken Soup for the Writer's Soul*, which included his story, and helped draw an enormous audience for us. Steve was enchanting, captivating, and funny as a speaker. He patiently and kindly answered everyone's questions and was delighted to sign every book. He died three days later, so it was his last signing.

I recommend that you always have too many titles, books, articles, reports, projects, and businesses to work on. It will keep your mind fully engaged, operative, and, ultimately, infinitely profitable. A master teacher said: "Greater is he or she that is in you than he that is in the world." It means what Thomas Alvin Edison said: "If you do all you are capable of, you will literally astonish yourself."

All the greats use their full talents. Bob Hope was a comedian, writer, actor, Broadway star, and radio personality. He won over 2,000 major awards, was a philanthropist, real estate investor, and was the richest man in Hollywood. However, he started out as a penniless immigrant from England. Be like Bob! You can have a rich, deep, meaningful, and fully functional life and lifestyle, and it will make you an infinitely better writer and person.

Writing books can be a little like raising children. There are advantages to growing up in a big family. Sometimes authors feel that working on multiple books will diminish their energy or concentration. The truth is probably just the opposite. If you're a real writer, you need to write—and when you're not writing, you can start to lose confidence in your creative identity. The solution? When, for whatever reason, you can't write the book you've been working on, work on a different book for a while. But keep working, because that's what you really want to do.

Cut the Beginning

One of the most ancient rules of writing is that the story should begin in the middle of things. *The Iliad*, the ancient Greek epic about the Trojan War, starts when the war has already been going on for ten years. What worked then still works now.

Likewise, when I record my books, I complete the entire recording and then go back and redo the first chapter. Why? Because I have gotten warmed up, hot in tune and tone, and energized, and I can do an infinitely better job. It is the nature of writing and talking that makes it so.

The playwright David Mamet makes this point in his book on the film industry, amusingly titled *Bambi versus Godzilla*. Mamet mentions how we can come into a movie or TV show ten or fifteen minutes after the start and still easily pick up the plot. In fact, it's kind of fun to do. The same principle works in other kinds of writing. The official introduction is almost disposable. When I read manuscripts by new writers, getting rid of the overture is always good advice.

If you've truly fallen in love with your opening, there's an alternative to getting rid of it completely. Try moving the opening a few paragraphs into the page, so that the second or third paragraph becomes the first. At the very least, this can be a good experiment. Let a few friends whose judgment you trust read both versions. You may be surprised by the result.

True, it can be hard to cut a paragraph you've worked hard on. But sometimes sacrifices have to be made for the greater good!

Nail the Table of Contents

When people talk about getting lost in a book, that's usually a good thing. They become so absorbed in what they're reading that they lose all sense of time and place. As writers, that's what we're after. However, there's a negative way in which a reader can get lost. It happens when readers lose confidence that the book knows where it's going or where it's been.

The problem usually begins before the first word is written. When a book's table of contents isn't completely thorough, it's going to cause problems. The table of contents should be logical, clear, and as simple as possible. Moreover, a few principles about how to create a decent table of contents seem to be wired into our brains. I'm not sure why they work, but they do.

This pertains mostly to nonfiction books. If you're writing a novel or a book of short stories, you have pretty much complete flexibility about the number of chapters or even whether there are chapters at all. But for nonfiction, there are a few rules that are written in stone.

Think about Word Count

When you submit your manuscript to an agent or a publisher, one of the most important pieces of information you'll need to provide is the number of words in your book. If, like almost everyone, you use Microsoft Word, getting that information is incredibly easy. There's a bar at the bottom of the page that tells you the exact word count of your document as it is now.

Many new writers don't know how many words will be in their book. They think in terms of pages. They say, "Oh, my book is about two hundred pages long." If you say something like that, you immediately tag yourself as an amateur.

Depending on how a book is formatted, a 30,000-word document can be the same size as one that is 50,000 words long. The massive best seller *Who Moved My Cheese?* is only 8,000 words long, but the dimensions of the book are identical to a book with a much higher word count. Generally speaking, publishers expect a non-fiction manuscript to be between somewhere between 60,000 and 100,000 words. Some very successful books are much shorter—Deepak Chopra's *The Seven Spiritual Laws of Success* is another example—but a new writer needs to provide something more substantial in terms of word count. The page count comes much later in the process.

Back Up the Files!

Writing a book is both a conscious and an unconscious process. Simply put, there's a lot of spooky stuff going on. If you're really putting your heart onto the page as you should, there will be a certain amount of inner resistance to the process. That resistance can surface in lots of unexpected ways. Plus, lots of other unexpected things can happen when a book is being written. So be prepared for some surprises!

Specifically, be ready for the possibility that, one way or another, you will actually lose the manuscript you've been working on—whether it's a hard copy or a computer file.

Does that sound impossible to you? Well, it probably seemed impossible to Ernest Hemingway too, until his wife left the only copy of his first book on a train. When John Milton's *Paradise Lost* was complete, his illiterate housekeeper burned the manuscript to stay warm. Devastated, he had to rewrite it from scratch. Milton was blind and, fortunately, is said to have had a perfect memory and retention. The same thing happened to Victorian essayist Thomas Carlyle and his manuscript on the French Revolution. So keep your work away from housekeepers!

The point here is simple: recognize that there's a lot of very sensitive energy present in your work in progress, and always be aware of how you'd feel if your only copy of that work suddenly disappeared. Back up your files. Send an email to yourself with the latest version of your book attached. I also send it to my executive assistant and editor. Keep it in the cloud and on a thumb drive or memory stick. Carry the memory stick with your book on it everywhere. That way you can continue to write more, and you'll have it if, God forbid, it disappears inadvertently from your computer.

You and I cannot afford the time to redo an entire book. Protect your work like this every day! Having your book disappear because of a computer glitch is an extremely unpleasant feeling, and that's putting it mildly. As for what it's really like—well, you don't want to find out for yourself.

Keep a Journal

Journaling used to something every educated person was supposed to do. President Ronald Reagan kept a journal every day. When you consider how busy a president is, that is an incredible feat. Reagan's published diaries makes for great, sensitive reading.

If you're a fan of Gene Rodenberry's *Star Trek*, as I am, note that Gene has Captain Jean-Luc Picard keep a daily journal, with each entry beginning: "Captain's log, star date 3010 AD." Even futurists journal, because no one can recall their entire life.

Looking at photos can help trigger your memories so you can better capture the essence and feelings of events as you write about them. Put some of your pictures in your journal. They can also be stored on your computer, or on different websites. In the past, journaling was seen as a matter of personal discipline. If some self-revelation took place along the way, that was just a positive side effect. But just because everybody was expected to do it doesn't mean that everybody did. Let's face it: for many people, journaling is not easy. Mark Twain joked about how impossible it is. But it really isn't impossible, and in terms of your writing career, journaling is definitely worth a serious try.

Oprah Winfrey has said there are two things that have shaped her life as an author. The first is her decision to read two books every week—which I hope you'll also do. Secondly, Oprah credits her commitment to journaling every day. Her journals ultimately became books, shows, magazine articles, and even businesses. She's received one of the highest advances ever for a book project. All this comes from her journals.

Unlike most people, Oprah doesn't write about what's already happened to her. Oprah journals her future. The more you journal your future—the more you put it right there on the page—the bigger and better, the brighter and grander, the more meaningful and powerful your future will be.

A Writing Secret from Detective Columbo

Just when you think your book is done, it's not done! This is a very important technique for ending your book with a big bang.

In Peter Falk's classic TV series, the rumpled detective Lieutenant Columbo always seemed to be letting the guilty party off the hook at the end of an interrogation—but just as he was opening the door to leave, he'd always turn slowly around and speak the fateful words: "Just one more thing . . ." Of course, "one more thing" always broke the case wide open.

You can break your book series wide open by gently seeding your reader's thinking toward what comes next. Lay the groundwork for the continuity of your books. This is something I learned from George Lucas's biography. He wouldn't write anything that he couldn't sequel and prequel. Wow! That concept dug deeply into my mind. I got it. What George did with *Star Wars*, I have done with my Chicken Soup for the Soul series, The One Minute Millionaire series, and *The Richest Kids in America* (which will become a series). Even the book you're reading now will be followed by many Speed Write books—see the list at the front of this book.

As you write your book, keep an inventory of your top ideas. Then save one of the very best for the last page of your finished manuscript. This can be designated as an epilogue, or it can just be part of your concluding chapter. But always leave the reader with a *wow* experience just before "The End."

Just Say, "Next!"

Louis L'Amour wrote more than one hundred Western novels and had 200 million books in print. He received three hundred and fifty rejections before he made his first sale.

Dr. Seuss' first children's book was rejected by twenty-five publishers. The twenty-eighth, Vanguard Press, sold 6 million copies of the book.

Fifteen publishers turned down John Grisham's first novel, *A Time To Kill.* More than 100 million copies of his books are now in print.

Star Wars, Forrest Gump, Home Alone, and *Pulp Fiction* were all initially rejected by major film studios.

In my seminars, I teach and preach that there is a clean four-letter word that overcomes all rejection: *next!* When Jack and I were turned down by 144 different publishers one by one, we just kept saying, "Next." Sooner or later, the law of attraction guarantees that we would synchronize in time and space with someone who would say, "Yes! We will be your publisher."

A small publisher in Deerfield Beach, Florida, had lost their main writer, Dr. John Bradshaw, and was having financial difficulties as a result—they were $17 million upside down. We knew none of this. However, the owners of this publisher, Health Communications, Inc., read our manuscript overnight. Gary Seidler and his partner,

Peter Vegso, said that as they read our book, they cried on their silk shirts. They said they would publish our book if we guaranteed to buy 20,000 copies at the exorbitant rate of $6 each, which we did. We wanted—and received—distribution on our terms.

PART TWO

Marketing Your Best Seller

People like to brag about their kids. It's just human nature. If your neighbor's son or daughter is named student of the month, you're going to hear about it over the backyard fence (although today you're more likely to read about it in an email or text message, complete with attached picture). It can be annoying when parents become too aggressive about this, but most people develop a certain amount of finesse. They find ways to let you know what's going on in their family without hitting you over the head with it.

What's this got to do with your career as an author? From the moment you finish writing your book, or even before you finish it, I want you to think of that book as your dearly beloved child.

A book is like your baby. You have a seed concept, it germinates inside you, and you go through the labor pains of writing it, delivering it, and sharing it with the world. In this process, you risk your self-esteem, and hope and pray that as you share your literary baby, it receives the loving reception it so richly deserves.

Motivate yourself to tell anyone and everyone about the exciting things your book is doing in the world. You must physically introduce your book to people, just as you would introduce your child to a new friend or acquaintance. In the same way parents learn to include their children in a conversation without being crass, you must learn how to introduce your book without overdoing it.

If you're having lunch with a group of friends, you won't talk about your book as if you were in front of an audience of three hundred people. But you *will* talk about your book. You *will* market your book 24/7/365 because (I have to say this one more time) the actual writing is only 10 percent of the book business; 90 percent is marketing, selling, promoting, sharing, telling, hustling and asking EVERYONE, EVERYWHERE, TO HELP YOU GET THE MESSAGE OUT IMMEDIATELY. Marketing, selling, and exposure on the largest possible scale: that's the other 90 percent.

There is a lot of noise—competition to be heard—in today's marketplace. It is said that over a million books a year in America are published, thanks largely to desktop publishing. YOU alone are responsible for being heard above the din and getting everyone to want to buy your book now.

When you meet people and they ask, "What do you do for a living?" proudly answer, "I am in the process of becoming a best-selling author." Tell them enthusiastically about your book. If the conversation warms up, ask if they can help you out. For example, inquire if they can send a note, text, or email (which you've already written and have with you) to friends. Ask if they know anyone in media that can help you secure a radio, television, newspaper, or online interview. Offer to talk to their group, company, podcast, social media or organization output.

Live, breathe, dream, think, and act with the knowledge that you are completely dedicated to making your baby a best seller.

Mention your book often during the day. Not every ten seconds, but as often as seems appropriate. Have a physical copy with you. Be ready to give it away.

One time I was changing planes in Salt Lake City, Utah, and bumped into one of the authors who inspired me to be a relentless book marketer. It was Dr. Wayne

Dyer, best known for the book *Your Erroneous Zones* (I used to help him carry and sell copies at his talks in metropolitan New York). Wayne, true to form, had his latest book in his backpack and said, "Mark, here's a gift of my newest book. Let me sign it for you and your family members. If you like it, and I know you will, please encourage everyone to get a copy."

Be eager to send your book out into the world. Do this both with friends and with people you've just met. Don't feel you have to ask for money, because very often the recipients of your book will want to pay for it. By all means, don't hesitate to accept that payment! This is your profession now. You're doing it as a business, not as a hobby.

Book profits (called royalties) are better than a salary. Once your book has momentum, you can receive endless payments. Think about L. Frank Baum, author of the classic Wizard of Oz books. His estate gets over $100 million annually in royalties on the Halloween costumes that sell every year, according to his estate attorney, who was mine for a while.

Remember, a book is a business. We will talk about this at length.

Of course, the real opportunities begin when you actually get up in front of a group or do a media outreach focusing on your book. We'll be talking more about how to make that happen throughout part 2.

When it does happen, make sure you're fully prepared. Watch a DVD of someone like the late motivational speaker Zig Ziglar in front of an audience. If Zig was marketing a book, it would always be in his hand. He'd keep lifting it up and showing it to the crowd as if it were a chalice full of holy water. He would talk about his book like a lifelong friend. He would tell stories, one after another, about his book. Zig would seem to baptize the audience with his book. He was continually marketing, but the emotion was so strong that it felt like something else entirely.

If you ever saw Zig at a giant rally with 10,000 people or more, you would see thousands of books stacked floor to ceiling as you entered the convention center. When you left, all the books would be sold, and the only things left were stack after stack of empty boxes. With practice, constant study, mentorship, and a white-hot burning desire, you can sell like Zig. Or do even better. It is enormously exciting and rewarding.

As you're becoming an expert marketer of your book, don't feel you have to do all the work by yourself. Recruit others to sell your book. Sales training is a huge industry, but you can train people yourself once you get some marketing experience. (At our zenith, we had many organizations busily selling our book through their respective sales teams to millions of people. Some of our many associates included: Reading Is Fun, Career Track, Skill Path, and Fred Pryor Seminars.) To paraphrase the Bible, once you seek, you will find many and varied opportunities to retail and wholesale your books.

Reading Is Fun from Fairfield, Iowa, had teams of salespeople going into schools to sell books to teachers and administrators. They were so hot that I went on several calls with them to see how they could sell so many.

Career Track from Boulder, Colorado, sold so much of our product that they paid Jack and me to come in and do a one-day seminar telling every story in our first book. A box of Kleenex was subtly placed under every seat in a fully sold-out auditorium of 5,000. They videotaped the entire event, showing stories such as John Corcoran's "The Millionaire Teacher Who Could Not Read." For a while, it became their best-selling video and audio program, and new and even greater royalty streams flowed to us. This is why in my book *The One Minute Millionaire*, I wrote that every multimillionaire has MSIs—multiple sources of income (a concept that I developed in 1988 and taught with Bob Proctor, head of Proctor Gallagher Institute).

One of our early breakthroughs was discovering a catalogue of catalogues. It was a catalogue that listed all the other catalogues that sold anything and everything. We wrote letters to all three hundred publications listed, and we made it into many of them. The one that is most memorable to me was the *Rose Bud Catalogue.* We were featured on the cover of the December issue (the best time to sell gift books like ours), surrounded by flowers, and it turned on an entire industry for us. For example, I was paid to give talks at 4 a.m. to flower growers in Albuquerque, New Mexico, before they took their flowers to market.

One thing is for sure: nobody knows more about your book than you do. When we were starting out with *Chicken Soup for the Soul,* we trained hundreds of representatives and lecturers for companies like Career Track to make calls for us. We trained them once a week by phone. It was scary, and I didn't feel confident doing it at first. Somehow I lived, the process worked, and books sold in volume. We made calls all over the world. I'd be talking to someone in Buenos Aries about the book, and somebody else would be calling Brazil. After a while, I looked at Jack Canfield and said, "You know what? I think this is going to work."

Invite everybody to sell your product. In early 2020, in the days of the coronavirus, my friend Harry Singer, owner of Ultra Soap products, told me that everyone was out of antiviral and antibacterial soap; 70 percent alcohol was also in short supply. Harry created a Survival antiviral and antibacterial soap box that started selling briskly on Amazon. Suddenly he was getting calls from hospitals desperate for his products. I asked him to insert an order form for my book *ASK! The Bridge from Your Dreams to Your Destiny.* It will be inserted into over 5,000 boxes a day. I think in the future, when we meet and you ask me, I will tell you that we cleaned up.

Speaking of packaging, Jack and I partnered with Campbell's Soup for packaging in a very literal way. They featured our books on every can's wrapper. We were on the inside wrapper with three Chicken Soup stories and an advertisement that was wrapped around 600 million Campbell's soup cans! The promotion benefited our readers, Campbell's favorite charity—the Andy Warhol Art Foundation in Pittsburgh—and our sales. Thanks to the vast and positive exposure, our book sales soared. Big opportunities like Campbell's take enormous amounts of time, planning, efforts, and communication. Yes, building such opportunities feels glacially slow sometimes, but is more than worth it if you are patient. Think of Job in the Bible. You can create opportunity by devoting a few minutes here and there to your cause, knowing all along that to make it happen is a monumental task and requires long-term desire.

Virtually every successful author has been an expert book marketer, especially in nonfiction. Don't try to be the exception to the rule. Just do it—and I'm going to show you how!

Write a WOW Business Plan

Before you begin writing a business plan, check out the competition. I interviewed 101 best-selling authors and asked them exactly how they approached marketing in the writing business. I interviewed both fiction and nonfiction authors, including M. Scott Peck, Wayne Dyer, Wally "Famous" Amos, John Gray, Ken Blanchard, Spencer Johnson, Wyland, Og Mandino, Zig Ziglar, Cavett Robert, Jeff Lant, Jean Houston, Barbara De Angelis, Deepak Chopra, Clive Cussler, Nora Roberts, and R. Buckminster Fuller. We copied their individual answers, condensed them onto little yellow Post-Its. Ultimately had 1,094 Post-Its on the wall of Jack's office in Culver City, California. We kept adjusting and moving them until they emerged as a WOW OF A BOOK BUSINESS PLAN. Try something like that yourself!

In the book business, there's a specialized document called a *book proposal.* I prefer to call it a business plan, because remember: you're not just writing a book, *you're going into the book business!* This is the first document that you will show to an agent, if you try to acquire one. It's also the first material pertaining to your book that an acquisitions editor will see. So it has to be a WOW both in terms of what it says, and in the professionalism it displays. It has to be eye-catching, original, different, interesting, unusual, and attention-grabbing—an impressive and well-packaged presentation. Today it is wise to include video and audio as well as podcast samples. The business plan is the platform that book buyers and publishers want to see that you can create with your name, fame, and brand. It really helps to be media savvy. Visit the website of Jillian Manus, my literary agent, at www.manuslit.com. Download and answer Jillian's ten questions. This questionnaire will help you think through your proposal.

Over the years, book proposals have followed a well-established format. Below I will show you a prime example. On the cover sheet of the document was a brief summary of the book—two or three short paragraphs—which functioned almost as an advertisement for the project. This was called the *overview.*

Then, on the first page of the document, was a bio of the author. This includes the author's previous books, the success of those books, and anything else about the author that might suggest his or her ability to connect with the widest possible audience. Be sure to mention you personal website here, and keep mentioning it multiple times within the book.

Building your website database for future data mining is immensely important for success in the book business, and you should never miss a chance to start doing that. In his book *Permission Marketing*, Seth Godin inspired me with an idea. Assume that you, like Clive Cussler or your favorite author, have a database of over 2 million raving fans who want to read everything you write. When you release a new book, you offer this list. Start with perhaps 200,000 copies in immediate sales at roughly $20 a copy. That's a gross of $4 million. Publishers will gladly give a million-dollar advance against first sales for those kind of results.

Following the bio is the table of contents for the proposed book. Remember, a clear, well-organized table of contents has always been vitally important and always will be!

As an extension of the table of contents, the proposal provides one-paragraph summaries of each chapter. There are also at least two *complete* chapters, written just as they would appear in the finalized book. Which chapters are included? The chapters the authors believe to be the strongest in terms of getting a publisher to buy their project.

Finally, the author provides his or her analysis of the market for the book. Which highly successful books are similar to this book? (When we were writing *ASK!*, because the first chapter was a parable, we compared it with *The Alchemist*, by Paulo Coelho, which had sold over 150 million copies over twenty-five years after being multiply rejected.) How can this new book connect with the same audience? Why will the book be even bigger than the biggest of the big?

At the end of the proposal, sometimes almost as an afterthought, is a description of what the author could do in terms of marketing the book. Radio interviews, book signings, and speaking events—the proposal concludes with the author's past experience with such marketing efforts and his or her hopes for the future. (Jack and I were speaking to over 250,000 people per year each.)

Well, that was then, even if "then" was just a few years ago. This is now! You've heard it said that the last shall be first? What used to be the last section of a book proposal—the description of the marketing savvy of the author—has now moved decisively up to the first position!

If you wish to release your book using the traditional mainstream paradigm of agent and publisher—as opposed to self-publishing or online release—you must, must, *must* be totally up to speed in your knowledge of marketing. What's more, you've got to have a platform that enables you to put your knowledge into action.

Simply put, your platform is the number of people who already know about you even before your book comes out. Hopefully, your platform is quite large; remember to keep saying you are a database builder, and build a database that *you* exclusively own. Your platform is the foundation upon which you will build even bigger numbers. The larger your platform, the more interest you'll receive from agents and publishers. And conversely, if you have no platform, you're probably going to get zero interest. As much as it hurts me to say it, this will often be true no matter how brilliant the content of your book might be. That's the book business, folks.

But wait! Suppose you bypass the traditional route and use one of the new self-publishing technologies. In that case, you'd better *really* know marketing, because there isn't even the pretense that a corporate publicist will take care of this for you. You're entirely on your own!

The good news is this: being on your own is absolutely the best place to be with regard to marketing—provided you thoroughly absorb the information I am about to share with you. In the book business as it exists today, your marketing savvy is the essence of your business plan. According to the late, great Dr. Peter Drucker, author and business advisor to corporations and governments, "There are only two profit centers in business: innovation and marketing." Your book, I have repeatedly said, must be original in both what's on the page and what's in the marketing. You must do things in marketing no one else has done before. Give your marketing the attention it deserves, which is *a lot*!

Have Giant Goals and Believe in Them

A verse in the Bible states, "Where there is no vision, the people perish" (Proverbs 29:19). I like to say: "With vision,

I flourish." I expect you to flourish and go beyond anything that has previously been done.

I actually prefer the word *vision* to the more common term *goals*. People can have goals for anything. You can set a goal for how much you eat or don't eat, for how much you sleep, or for how much you spend or earn. But vision is of a higher order. Vision suggests an emotional and spiritual connection. That's what you need for your book: a vision that the book will change many lives, maybe even the entire world. Our vision for Chicken Soup: "Change the whole world, one story at a time."

Many books have changed and continue to change the world. They include *Relativity* by Albert Einstein; *An Essay on Population* by Thomas Malthus; *The Interpretation of Dreams* by Sigmund Freud; *I Seem to Be a Verb* by R. Buckminster Fuller; *Huckleberry Finn* by Mark Twain; and *The Alchemist* by Paulo Coelho.

Does that seem like a tall order? For a writer, it's much better to aim too high than too low. You've got to dramatize your work in your own mind just as you've got to dramatize your subject on the page.

As we begin this section on marketing, I want you to create of vision of your book at the top of the *New York Times* best-seller list! This is the list bookstores, libraries, and reading clubs use to make their buying decisions.

As I've already said, it's a good idea to cut the list out of this Sunday's *New York Times* and paste your title and name at the top. Tape it to your bathroom mirror so that you look at it every morning, again at noon, before dinner, and, most importantly, just prior to bed. The best time to program your mind is just before going to sleep. Your brain will accept the positive input that you are the number-one author on the *New York Times* best-seller list, and will work all night long with that information. I will keep repeating the critical importance of programming your mind for success. Your book and its marketing represent a vision you're going to turn into a reality. It's a vision that's going to, both figuratively and literally, enrich both you and the world.

Plan to Write More than One Book

When Jack Canfield and I started talking about writing books together, we definitely intended to write than one. How many did we plan? Two or three? Actually, as previously mentioned, we came up with 134 titles.

I expect to live to be 127 years old, with options for renewal! Therefore I keep finding new collaborators. Daily I am offered juicy potential assignments. I have a long list of what I want to do. What's amazing to me is how many people ask why I don't retire. As my friend Willie Nelson suggests, "What does one retire from or to? I love writing, singing, traveling, performing, working on stage with my family. Seeing 140 shows per year. Golfing during the day and performing at night. I own two giant ranches. I beat the IRS. Playing cards with my friends. Raising money for charities that I believe in. And I wrote and sang the laughable hit, *Roll Me Up and Smoke Me When I Die.* I have a gloriously fulfilling life. If retirement is being happy and leisurely, I am that now at 86 years old and having the time of my life."

I have read over 5,612 biographies and autobiographies and recommend this practice to you. I read Isaac Asimov's autobiography because I had read so many of his phenomenal books, which covered a variety of subjects, as mentioned above. On the night we wrote all those titles, I told Jack that Asimov, one of our mutual writing heroes, had written over five hundred best-selling books. I innocently and positively declared, "We can do the same and, who knows, maybe more!"

Big plans yield big results. Little plans get *no* results, because they don't hit you at the depth of your abilities, inspire self-initiative action, or challenge you at a soul level. The gods of writing have a lot to think about. You've got to do something that will grab their attention. Little plans won't do it. Little plans mean you don't really care. Or maybe it's even worse. Little plans mean you don't feel like using the millions and millions of amazing brain cells that you've been given—because you just don't get how important you are or how beneficial your work can be for other people. So start getting it! I give you full and absolute permission to manifest your greatness in writing, business, and all of life.

Do you have some idea that's been roaming around in your head for a while—a story that you'd like to tell, whether fiction or nonfiction? A message that you know you've been called upon to share with the world—although, for whatever reason, you just haven't done it yet? Maybe it's only a few notes that you've scribbled down on a piece of paper. But it's not a real book yet. It's not even an outline. Don't beat yourself up for not having gotten any further. In fact, you should congratulate yourself for having taken the all-important first step of coming up with an idea.

Then come up with *more* ideas! For the time being, don't worry about executing them. Just brainstorm about the books you plan to write and how you'll get them out into the world. Make sure you put them all in writing.

Begin with Your Ultimate Success in Mind

I'm sure you've heard it said that a journey of 1,000 miles begins with a single step. True enough! With regard to marketing your book, that means seeing every contact, every phone call, every email, text, and even every rejection as a step toward the megasuccess you have in mind.

This takes a little bit of mental gymnastics. You need to think small and big at the same time. You need to see the end *from* the beginning. The preposition *from* is critical, because you have to *be* there before you *get* there. The Bible says, "I call those things that are not as though they were, and they came into being."

The end is always present in the beginning. That's how the world works. Look at an acorn. Can you see the oak tree inside it? Is it really possible that something so small can turn into something so big? The truth is, it's not only possible; it's *inevitable*, provided you create the right conditions for nature to take its course. The deed is in the seed. The deed is the result of your seed thinking. Think as if you already are the author that you will be—and you will be that author.

The same principle holds for getting your book to the world. At the start, your book was nothing. It was just an intangible idea in your mind. Then it was a word on a page. First one word, then a second, and, finally, tens of thousands of them. Eventually your book becomes a physical object you can hold in your hand.

Now your task is to take the same process that enabled you create something out of nothing and translate it into the larger world. Just as you once saw the blank page as the acorn of your literary oak tree, now you should see the single volume on the table in front of you as millions of books on millions of tables.

Do you have that vision in mind? Good. Now make just *one* phone call that will bring that vision closer to reality.

Reject Rejection

How can you tell if you're going to make it in the book business? One thing virtually all successful writers seem to have in common is a period—often a long period—of nothing but rejection. Stephen King tossed the opening four chapters of *Carrie*, his first novel, into the wastebasket. His wife found them, read them, and urged him to go on with the book. The rest, as they say, is history.

It's eerie how almost exactly the same thing happened to Dr. Norman Vincent Peale and Irving Stone, author of *The Agony and the Ecstasy* and many other great historical novels. Both of them had stories involving an early manuscript, a wastebasket—and a wife!

There are many variations on this theme. TV anchor Ted Koppel said he could have wallpapered his apartment with the rejection notices he received in his pursuit of work as a foreign correspondent. One of my favorite stories is about singer Amy Grant. When she launched her first album, there was going to be a big signing in the record store. The record company sent out eighteen hundred hand-engraved invitations. A full house was expected. Not one person showed up. She sang for ninety minutes to the store manager.

As Jack and were repeatedly getting rejected, we kept saying, "Next!" If you say, "Next!" long enough, someone will eventually and inevitably say yes. Remember, Jack and I received 144 rejections before a small publisher in Deerfield Beach, Florida said, "We will take it if you promise to buy 20,000 copies at $6 each." That was a vanity press, and I advise against using these, but we were desperate, and we accepted what today looks like an absurd offer. We made the owner of Health Communications, Inc., rich and famous. He claims he made *us*, which makes me laugh.

Rejection is not fun, but I learned to treasure the experience. Once you get your head around it, rejection can encourage you. It can even inspire you. As the disappointments piled up, I thought, "You know what? If I just hang in there, I'm going to get this message out to the world." It was a conscious decision to *not* think about how long it would take or how much work it would involve. I didn't care if I was eighty years old when it finally happened, because it *was* going to happen. And it *did* happen.

Now I'm glad to be in the company of best-selling authors who learned to reject rejection. I look forward to welcoming you to that very select group!

Use Matrix Multiples

Let's take a look at one good way to turn something small (your book) into something really big (your book as an international best seller.) Suppose you've written an insider's guide to being a commercial airline pilot. You've decided to self-publish the book, and you're thinking about how many copies you should get printed.

With the amazing print-on-demand capabilities available today, you don't have to roll the dice when you decide on your first print run. Instead, go online and visit the website of the airline pilots union. You learn that the union has 50,000 members. The real figure may be more or less than that, but let's stick with 50,000 for our purposes. With a little creative thinking, you come up with an article that's appropriate for the union's website, submit it to the site's webmaster, and, because you're such a good writer, the article gets posted. Of course—no surprise here—the article mentions your book, and the fact that it's available through Amazon.

Things are looking good. Over the next few weeks, your book sells five hundred copies through Amazon. Now you've got an idea of how much interest you can expect to generate from a qualified database like the pilots' union website.

So you take the next step, which is visiting the website of the association of *retired* airline pilots. You've moved from one matrix to a second one. The second one happens to be considerably larger than the first, because there are more retired airline pilots than active ones. Once again you come up with an article for the website, and this time you use your first article as part of your pitch for the second one. Again your article is accepted for posting, with the link to Amazon.

As a result, you sell more books, you expand your résumé as a writer, and you continue thinking about larger and larger matrices through which you can market your book. Flight attendants, airline passenger groups, pilots in training, anybody and everybody who has any connection with air travel. Use each matrix as a stepping-stone to a larger one. With each step, you'll become more knowledgeable about how many copies, what kind of offers, and everything else you need to fully access your expanding database.

Go to BEA

Regardless of where you are in the creation of your book business, you should definitely attend the publishing industry's annual convention, Book Expo America (BEA). It's held on the first weekend after Memorial Day, usually in New York (be sure to check, because meetings are morphing with venue and personnel availability). The 60,000 attendees include publishers, agents, authors, distributors, ghostwriters, and many other book industry professionals. Attending BEA will expand your understanding of the publishing industry as a $25 billion colossus.

When we were first starting to market *Chicken Soup for the Soul*, I had never heard of this convention. Then

Jack Canfield called and said, "Mark, we've got to go to the book expo." We had just been on the road for a solid month, with more traveling to come. That weekend was my only time off, so I was not very eager to attend a trade show. My wife did not exactly like the idea either, but Jack was emphatic. He said, "We'll just go for two hours."

So we went, and I thought I had died and gone to heaven. Authors, speakers, thinkers, artists, poets, publicists, cartoonists, movie directors like Steven Spielberg, TV stars like Oprah Winfrey, and even former president Jimmy Carter were there. My soul was deeply wowed. I was ecstatic. These were my people! We were making new contacts, swapping business cards, and taking pictures with celebrities like Oprah. Most importantly, we were directly soliciting publishers to take on our book and distribute it. We were hungry for a deal, and expectant of finding one.

That year the BEA was in Anaheim, just south of Los Angeles. We had packs full of three-ring binders with the manuscript for *Chicken Soup for the Soul.* I didn't know we were going to get rejected all day long, and even if I had known, I'm not sure I would have cared—because when I walked into that convention, I could not believe my eyes.

I was expecting a quiet literary event, but was immediately hit by a stunning revelation. I realized that a book is much more than just a book. A book is one expression of an idea that can have many different manifestations. Everything eventually turns into a book, and a book eventually turns into everything else. Every movie is a book. Every play is a book. Every story is a book. Every song is a book. That's why it seemed like everybody who was anybody was at the BEA. Muhammad Ali was there. Charles Schulz, the "Peanuts" cartoonist, was there. Over that three-day weekend, 60,000 people were at the convention. We were able to meet them, get pictures with them, and have fun with them—and we also got lots of free books! Inside the convention center there was even a UPS booth where you could quickly mail your stash of books home.

There are countless opportunities at the BEA. Attending the convention every year is really a vital part of professionalizing yourself in the book business. Don't be intimidated by the size of the event, the "who's who" in attendance, or the parties that last all night long.

Instead take advantage of all the opportunities. Decide you belong there. Enjoy yourself. Bring someone with you, and live it up. I give you permission. Carry your charged-up smartphone to record all your favorite authors' words for you. Have your journal in your computer bag or purse. And by all means bring your WOW OF A BOOK BUSINESS PLAN. Bring multiple copies!

Meet as many people as you can, talk about your book, and pay attention to what you hear. By the end of the weekend, you'll be looking at your project in a whole new way. It won't be just something that's happening at your kitchen table anymore. Over the course of three days, you'll meet selling authors and leave feeling that you can outthink, outwrite, outsell, and outperform many of them! This will enormously boost your confidence and your belief in yourself.

Sign Books!

I once walked into bookstore in a Los Angeles mall, and John Gray, author of *Men Are from Mars, Women Are from Venus*, was there doing a book signing. This was just as his books were starting to take off, and not many fans were present. But the energy John projected was amazing. He couldn't have been more enthusiastic if there were 5,000 people waiting in line. As a potential best-selling author, you'll want to keep this example in mind. You need to be the master of your energetic output, and give 100 percent, even if only three people show up. One of those people may be your ticket to best-seller status. You never know who someone is or how he or she can help you. So be committed to do whatever it takes to succeed and prosper as an author.

Be aware that, beyond giving you the opportunity to do a book signing, a bookstore can't be relied upon to bring in the audience. That will be up to you, and you should try to get the word out to as many people as possible. Send emails to everybody you know. Make the emails direct and to the point: "This is where I'm going to be, and this is when I'm going to be there. PLEASE COME, AND BRING ALL YOUR FRIENDS, NEIGHBORS, RELATIVES, AND COLLEAGUES FROM WORK!"

Design an invitation or bookmark, print a thousand of them, and ask the store to give one away with every purchase starting two weeks before the event. Get the store to put a big sign in the window. Make the sign yourself! Above all, befriend the bookstore owner. Every one I've met has been great. By and large, book people are bright, friendly, and easy to talk to.

Signings don't always draw a huge audience, but they're an excellent way to gain valuable experience talking about your work. It's also an opportunity to create a positive relationship with storeowners, managers, and salespeople who will happily recommend your book. (This is called hand-along sales.) You simply have to be nice to them, befriend them, and ask them to help you with customers they meet.

Become a Sought-after Expert

In the past, it took years to become an expert on anything. Information was much harder to come by. If you wanted to learn about a subject in depth, you had to spend months checking books out of the library or enroll in a course in a college or university. Sometimes you could take a correspondence course, but finishing it could take the rest of your life. Even if you did gain expertise in a particular topic, becoming recognized as an authority could be even more difficult and time-consuming. Some of the greatest experts in many different fields were probably totally unrecognized. Nobody knew about them.

Today, because of the Internet, it takes about one week of focused attention to become very well informed about virtually any topic in the world. In two weeks you can gain knowledge that used to take a lifetime to acquire. If you read five books on a subject with good to great retention—and with focus and genuine interest—you will be more knowledgeable than 80 percent of the people in the field. If you keep reading books and periodicals on the topic for six months to one year, you can be considered an expert on that topic. It has never been easier to master a subject.

The Four-Hour Work Week was written by Tim Ferris. (Jack Canfield mentored Tim.) It became an instant best seller because it made a promise that interested everyone who wants time freedom. That includes most of us. Tim suggests that everyone who really wants to can quickly become sufficient, proficient, and efficient in virtually any subject. The more areas you master, the faster you can master the next subject, and the next, and the next.

Obviously, as a writer, you want to become a lifelong reader, student, and learner. But that's only the beginning. Once you've become an expert, you can immediately make the world aware of that fact. You can join website groups, contribute to blogs, or start a website or a blog of your own.

It behooves you to immediately identify and communicate with the greatest authorities in the field you've chosen. Every field has lots of people in it, but only ten, at the most, are the reigning greats. Contact them by mail, email, or in person. Most people will generously help a sincere and respectful newcomer.

As you begin to establish these relationships, something really amazing will happen. Instead of you seeking people out, people will start to seek *you* out. You'll start getting emails and text messages asking for your opinion, and you may even be asked to appear at live events. When that happens, you're going to be able to sell plenty of books!

I commenced my speaking career training and talking every day in the life insurance business. I listened to every audio done by the Million Dollar Round Table, General Agents and Managers Association, and every one of the companies that I worked for. I listened and took notes at every life insurance convention. I met and befriended all the greats and the company leaders. Amazingly, as I write this, looking back on my phenomenal experiences, the leaders in the industry are planning to combine the East and the West's life underwriters from around the world and cooperate in a major way. They have asked me to write the book that my wife titled, *Sell Like the Greats!* It will be a joy again to interview and write about the giants in the profession. It is one of my next big tasks.

Insurance creates wealth with a few drops of ink and a piece of paper called a *life contract*. It has created billions of new dollars with well-packaged ideas. I have learned from industry giant John Savage that there are four wheels to financial freedom: earnings, savings, investments, and life insurance. It will be a joy to create and write this book.

Use Remnant Space Ads

Print advertising can be expensive, but there's a great way to get started with virtually no front-end cost.

Magazines depend on advertising to survive. If there aren't enough ads, there's no publication. It's that simple. So let's say there's a magazine that's 200 pages long. Each issue has to have at least 100 pages of advertising. But suppose they don't sell 100 pages of advertising in a given month. That definitely happens, and for you it can be an excellent opportunity.

You can create a remnant space ad, which is simply an ad that fills up the space that would otherwise be blank. These are called P.I. (per inquiry) ads. You pay a percentage of your book's sale price—10 to 50 percent, depending on your negotiation abilities—to the magazine, and you fulfill the book order. This possibility is not advertised and is not common knowledge, so befriend the head of advertising sales or a magazine editor—and voilà, you can discover the possibilities for deals. There are people who specialize in P.I. advertising. Now that you know what you're looking for, you can find them. The spiritual law is, "Seek and you will find."

Content Is King and Distribution Is Queen!

On the Internet, there are many ways to spread the word about who you are and your area of expertise. You want to maximize all those opportunities. You'll be surprised how fast this can happen, with just a bit of effort on your part to get the ball rolling.

If you're successful with your podcast, blog, or vlog, if you provide value to people on a consistent basis so that they keep coming back, your content will automatically start to spread to other locations on the web. It'll be discussed on Twitter, talked about on Facebook, and maybe filmed for YouTube. We'll discuss this further in part 3.

There are a couple other ways to get the word out. You can use Friend Feed—a feed aggregator that consolidates the updates from social media and social networking websites, social bookmarking websites, blogs, and microblogging updates, as well as any other type of RSS/Atom feed. I strongly suggest that you write a couple of free articles about your topic for sites, because the web will repurpose these articles, or in other words, spread them around to various websites that need more information on your topic as filler. This will start to establish you as an expert in the eyes of your readers and of Google.

In terms of Internet validation for the search engines, it is actually more important that other people link to you than you link to other people, so when you create content of value—that is, it's funny, educational, interesting, or inspiring—people will start to create links to your website and your blog, and the word will get around. On YouTube, a video can go from zero to millions of views overnight. It's just a matter of creating something that's interesting and meaningful to as many viewers as possible.

I also encourage you to connect your topic to topics in the media that get buzz. Mentioning celebrities, major events in history, and famous works of art, literature, and music tends to draw more people your way, which is especially useful if your topic is obscure.

In all of your blog entries, provide resource links to two external sites. For example, if you wrote a book about how to reduce debt, you don't want to have three links to Amazon to buy your book without any other interesting links. Provide links in the body of the blog to send people to helpful resources, like an article in the *Times* on becoming debt-free, or to Wikipedia to learn about the origin of money. Then at the end of your blog, invite people to check out your book. That way you're providing value to people, so they appreciate what you are *offering* rather than just *selling*. The paradox is this: when people feel you are delivering value for free, they'll be much more likely to spend their money on your book.

Become Supercharitable

One of my earliest books, now in its third edition, is *The Miracle of Tithing*, in which I taught the four ways of giving: (1) your thinking, (2) your talents, (3) your time, and (4) your treasures, with the bonus being your thankfulness for all the abundance you experience and express.

From the beginning, Jack and I have tithed on every Chicken Soup book. We've donated at least 10 percent of our income from every book to charitable causes. First and foremost, that's been a very important thing to do because it's healthy for the soul, it brings about tangible benefits in the world, and, depending on what you get involved with, it can really make a difference. Think about microlending, or microcredit. This is a very small amount of money loaned to a person or a family in poverty to help spur entrepreneurship. It works worldwide. You don't have to know how to end world hunger. You can figure out how to get one goat, or one dollar, to someone who needs it, and the difference begins there.

Two resources on the subject are my *Miracle of Tithing*, and former president Bill Clinton's book *Giving*. Also, learn about Muhammad Yunus, who has taken 100 million women out of poverty with microlending and won a Nobel Peace Prize. He's definitely one of my heroes.

Even if you haven't written your book yet, start thinking about a cause in the world that you feel passionately about. Identify it now. I don't care what your church, charity, or spiritual disposition is. If we have a network of enlightened millionaires dedicated to doing good around the world, imagine how much could get done—and how fast!

I am personally dedicated to making that happen. Bill Gates and Warren Buffet created and launched the First Supper (after the Last Supper), and they asked all billionaires to pledge to give away 50 percent of their enormous wealth while still alive. I gather that Warren says that it is working much better than expected.

I hope you will be inspired by my words, actions, and thinking to be a lifelong contributor. Helen Keller said, "Alone we can do so little; together we can do so much."

If all writers started giving a percentage of their profits to worthy causes, readership would boom and bloom, and sales would skyrocket. Prolific writers might even write a book and contribute *all* the profits to a cause they believe in. In turn, this could create a legacy that would go on forever. John Demartini, my great friend, a specialist in personal development, and a superb writer, believes that each of us needs to leave a thousand-year legacy of contribution. He says, "Think not about mortal goals, but immortal goals." I hope that thought inspires you!

Sociologist Margaret Mead said, "Never doubt that a small group of thoughtful, committed citizens can change the world. Indeed, it is the only thing that ever has." All it takes is a few good men and women changing their mental direction to change the direction, compass, and ultimate destination of the world.

Plato said, "Those who tell stories rule the world."

Depending on where you are in your career, you may hesitate. You might not feel you can afford to expend a certain percentage of your income on charity. But that's a big mistake. First of all, just on a tactical level, getting involved with philanthropic endeavors is going to put you in touch with a lot of people you'd never meet if you stuffed your money into a Prince Albert can, a bank, or your mattress. Those people might really help you.

Second, if you tell yourself that you can't afford to be charitable, you are falling into the trap of scarcity consciousness, which will not help you generate abundance. Scarcity thinking repels abundance. See my best seller

The One Minute Millionaire (the proposal for which I've included below), and give yourself the advantage of a prosperous mental attitude.

Being charitable makes you *feel* richer, and that alone will generate more abundance in your life. It's a matter of expanding your sense of self so you feel magnanimous instead of constricted. If you feel uncomfortable giving money, you can always give a little of your smile, friendship, kindness, and old clothes to Goodwill or the Salvation Army. Consider reading my book *Chicken Soup for the Volunteer's Soul*, and get yourself out there in a giving way.

Create a Vlog, Blog, or Podcast First (*Not* a Website)

Everyone in every business knows that the Internet has changed everything, and everyone is eager to take advantage of that fact, right? So far, so good—but there's a right way and a wrong way to use that advantage.

For most people, and certainly for most new authors, the wrong way is to create a really beautiful (and really expensive) website. That's a big mistake for several reasons. First, the key to every form of Internet success is to constantly update your site, and that's not always easy to do with a conventional website. So you either have to devote time and energy to learning how to do it yourself or you have to hire someone to do it for you. When you add the cost of creating the website in the first place, you can be far in the red before you even get started. Nevertheless, today there are lots of relatively inexpensive ways to do it.

A vlog, blog, or podcast, on the other hand, can be either very inexpensive or free, and is also much easier to update than a full-fledged website. Vlogs, blogs, and podcasts may not be beautiful, but they're much more dynamic. It's generally not feasible to sell your book directly through your vlog, blog, or podcast, but it's easy to provide a link to www.amazon.com that will accomplish the same thing.

Use Your Vlog, Blog, or Podcast to Build a Database

The greatest asset a vlog, blog, or podcast can provide is your database—which is simply the email addresses of people who visit it. You'll want to do everything you can to capture those email addresses, because these are the people you will turn into long-term customers.

Most visitors to your blog will not volunteer to give you their email addresses. You can have a clickable icon that asks visitors to join your blog's online community by signing in with their email address, but most of them won't do it. Why should they, if they're not getting anything in return? That's why you should offer something for free: a sample chapter of your book, a special article, tickets to your seminar or event, a group conversation, a private and exclusive event, or a small but meaningful and desirable gift. In the industry, this is called an *air gift.* The cost to you is zero or negligible when compared to the dollars earned. It is an ethical bribe, according to Jay Abraham, the world's greatest marketer.

Viewers can download their gift in exchange for their email address. Or give them a discount on the full purchase price if they create a membership on your site.

Better yet, give them both a sample chapter and a discount. Remember: the first and foremost goal is to *build your database.* The more free stuff you can provide, the faster that database will build. Don't think of it as a giveaway. Think of it as an investment, because that's exactly what it is. I see *Chicken Soup for the Soul* readers as lifelong customers and friends. The emotional impact and connection of our stories keeps them coming back for more. Our stories cause memorable, instant, and powerful inner change.

Bob Allen and I melted down Jeff Bezos, when we watched him challenge us on TV by saying: "No one can sell more books than Amazon can deliver."

Bob had just been enormously successful with his challenge for his book *Nothing Down.* Bob had said, "Send me to any city, and I will buy $1 million worth of real estate starting with $100." Bob was videoed by the media doing just that in San Francisco.

Next he said, "Send me into any unemployment line and I will get everyone earning $5,000 a month within a month, or I will pay them that amount." Again, he did it. So when we watched Jeff make that outrageous statement, I said, "Bob, I think he is challenging us." We agreed, and we decided to figure out how to sell more and faster than he could deliver.

Bob Allen and I launched *The One Minute Millionaire* on October 17, 2001 (before spam laws). We partnered with Ancestry.com. Ancestry sent out 3 million emails to their faithful clients recommending that if they bought our book from Amazon between 6 a.m. and 11 p.m. that day, they would get $250 worth of Bob's and $250 worth of my electronic products. As I remember, at 6 a.m. we were at number 79,000 on Amazon's book selling lists. By 10 a.m., we were at 750, and Amazon's underprepared and overburdened systems came screeching to a halt. Three hours later, Jeff Bezos called and said, "I will give you three first-class round trip tickets to my Seattle headquarters to tell us how you did it."

Bob Allen, Tom Painter—our inside promoter, strategist, and operation guy—and I went. It was delightful fun. If we had known he'd become the world's richest man and Amazon would become the Everything Store, we would have asked more questions and taken videos and pictures to commemorate, publicize, and immortalize our success.

When You're Ready for Your First Website

As your vlog, blog, and podcasts gains some traction and you start to develop a following, you will want to create a website for yourself and your book where you can post PR, reviews, daily social media videos, testimonials, and information about your books, book tours, and speaking engagements.

Remember: You must know and stay on top of the three best websites in your area of expertise. These change constantly. You need to know what is working now on a website, why it's working, and how you can use it to make your own website more active and appealing.

Make Maximum Use of Your Database

Your database is gold. Today people talk about data mining. Your goal is to create a giant and ever expanding data list to mine and remine forever. Let me tell you a little secret: you won't make the most money by selling your book—unless you sell millions and millions of copies, or have a book that sells for $1,000 per copy and you sell over 1,000 copies (yes, books like that do exist!). You are going to make your real money from your database. How?

Your database contains the people who will also buy the next five books you write, attend your retreat, and enroll for your telecourse. Basically, your database can put your kids through college. But this will only happen if you maintain a meaningful relationship with your database members over the years.

Your database finds suspects, qualifies them as prospects, turns them into customers with their first purchase, and ultimately converts them into clients and raving fans who want to read everything you have written. I, for example, have read everything by Napoleon Hill, Bob Allen, Bob Proctor, Sydney Sheldon, Michael Crichton, Clive Cussler, R. Buckminster Fuller, and many other authors who populate my personal library.

Handle your database delicately. It is possible to burn out an enormous database with a few careless choices on your part. It is also possible to have a small database that purchases everything you publish because they are crazy about your work. It is not about numbers; it *is* about temperature.

In the book business, we refer to your database as your *list*, and lists are either hot or cold. You want a hot list. In other words, you want to talk to your list on a regular basis, providing tons of value, and continually build your list without seeing people unsubscribe from it.

How do you do that? Start with your friends and family, and then begin collecting the emails of every person you meet and entering them into your database. Also, create an opt-in box on your website or blog. People who check that box will then start receiving your newsletter. Always give them the option to opt out if they want.

By using your database, you can also introduce or promote other people who have a message that would be meaningful to your list. For example, if you have written a book about divorce, you might include in your newsletter an article written by a friend about communicating to kids during the end of a marriage. Your list will probably appreciate the article, and your friend gets a little more exposure. It's a win-win situation.

A good thing sells itself. If you provide value—like free tips and information to your database—they'll keep coming back, they'll tell their friends about you, and your database will grow. But if you try to sell them to death, it won't matter if there are a million people on your list. They will not want to buy anything from you, and your list will become cold.

Treat your database as you would treat your best friends. Be respectful, fun, playful, and basically be yourself. People will be drawn to you if you simply keep providing value!

Get Your Book Reviewed—Everywhere, Anywhere

It's not hard to get your book reviewed—you can't just review it yourself! But don't let that stop you, and don't think you have to limit your reviewing possibilities to *The New York Times* either. In fact, don't even limit yourself to print media. You want to get your book reviewed in as many places and in many ways as is humanly possible.

Here are a few ideas to get you started.

First, take a proactive approach. If you've been doing a good job of getting your book out into the world, it is already in the hands of your friends and family. There's no reason why these people can't become your first reviewers—not for the national media, but for community newspapers and newsletters, or for any other outlet that's seen by even a small number of people. No matter how tiny that number may be, it's definitely going to be bigger than zero.

It's best if a potential reviewer sends an inquiry to the editor of the publication before actually writing the text, since the editor will probably offer some valuable advice about style and word count. Don't feel the slightest bit uneasy about enlisting a friend to write a positive review on your behalf. This is how the game is played—not just on the beginner's level, but all the way to the top. When you get there, you'll see just how true that is.

Use One Hard-hitting Chapter as a Marketing Tool

This one is counterintuitive. You want people to buy your book, so you actually need to give some of it away for free. It sounds crazy, right? Why will people buy something when they can get it for free? But they do it every day. Think about walking down the aisle of the supermarket, and there is a woman giving away free samples of corn chowder. You came to buy milk, but you taste the corn chowder.

How can you refuse? It's free! And you like it, and think your mother might like it, so you find yourself walking out of the store with a carton of milk and two cans of corn chowder. How did that happen? Someone gave you a taste for free.

In 1983 Tom Peters published *In Search of Excellence*, the first of an entirely new generation of business books. The book was written during the first big gasoline crisis in the late seventies, when there was a sense that America couldn't do anything right. Peters, a business consultant and a former professor, studied a small number of companies that were financially successful and had very high-quality products. He looked at what they were doing right and why. His publisher planned to print 10,000 copies, but Peters himself photocopied an additional 15,000 copies and sent them to as many people as he could think of. He gave thousands of books away. The publisher was furious! However, *In Search of Excellence* became an all-time best seller. The book created a platform for writing additional best sellers, which I have eagerly read, because Tom is a courageous and original thinker and speaker. He has become a high-priced, irreverent, and insightful commentator, and I encourage you to visit his website at www.tompeters.com.

A flashbook is another excellent option for providing free content to your readers. A flashbook is a video clip containing a small selection of images and text overlaid onto ten to twelve PowerPoint slides, with fabulous music to accompany it. A flashbook about *The Dash: Making a Difference with Your Life,* has attracted millions and millions of views. You can see it at www.simpletruths.com. Mac Anderson, who owns Simple Truths, sent out 30,000 copies of the flashbook offering the hardcover book for $16.95. As of this writing, there have been more than 45 million views of *The Dash*, with 5.5 million copies of the book sold.

An effective flashbook contains three elements:

1. The wow factor. You immediately think, "This is great!"
2. It captures your emotional attention from the first second to the last, for a total run time of three minutes or less.
3. It tells a compelling story that you will remember and want to share with your friends.

Whether you're giving away one chapter or sending out a flashbook, you want certain responses from the people you contact. You want them to buy your book. You want them to give you their email address so they become part of your database. And you want them to keep coming back and telling all their friends to do the same. For most enterprises, 80 percent of their business is return customers. That means that you, the seller, will create a meaningful, ongoing relationship with your customers. Whatever you choose to give away, it needs to be something people can download easily and enjoy immediately. It should also tell people how they can purchase the rest of the book and sign up for your free newsletter. If you do this correctly, the value you provide will create lasting and trusting relationships with your customers.

Create a Newsletter

I mentioned that having a customer means having a relationship with that customer, and there is no better way to accomplish this than to create an email newsletter. The sites today are very affordable, and they manage your database as well as your newsletters. You might even have signed up for a few email newsletters yourself. Some of them are extravagant and offer tons of bells and whistles so that you can see how many people opened your newsletter or clicked through to what you offer. Some are text only and can get through any spam filter. Constant Contact, Campaigner, AWeber, Namaste Interactive, and iContact are great online resources for starting your own newsletter.

You can choose to send out your newsletter once a week, once a month, or just randomly, depending on your style. However you go about it, make sure it's fun for you and for your readers. Don't just blast them with sales messages. I know a woman who writes a newsletter to help other writers find funding sources. In every issue, she includes a photo of herself with her elderly, blind dachshund. Her subscribers love her dog and always enjoy hearing about him in every letter. Personal details help people connect with you. They get to know you and trust you. That's at least as important for your book sales as giving them a link to Amazon.

What about Branding?

Branding is a buzzword in the book business that you are going to hear a lot. As an author, you want to be branded. All it means is that you create something that is recognizable to people so that they know what you stand for. Tom Peters says, "Be distinct or extinct!" You might choose certain colors or images, but all of that is secondary to the experience you take to people.

Think about Volvo for a moment. That's a very popular brand of car. What do you think of when you hear Volvo? Probably safety. That is how they have branded themselves. Consider the Nike swoosh symbol, or even the Italian flag, which is just three colors side by side; green, white, and red. These are all examples of branding. As you get your website and your book cover put together, write down three words that express the feeling and the experience you want to convey. Those words will become your brand.

Jack and I have been very successful with our Chicken Soup brand. People know that when they pick up one of our books, they are going to feel inspired and connected. Our books are immediately and easily distinguishable from every other book out there. Make no mistake: there is a power in a brand that commands. If you want your book to stand out, check the video available on my website called Building a Brand That Commands.

Read *1001 Ways to Market Your Book* by John Kremer

This book is the bible of creative book marketing. It is composed of quick chapters that offer easy-to-do, affordable, and actionable items that you can implement today.

Now in its sixth edition, *1001 Ways to Market Your Book* includes nearly seven hundred pages of helpful advice and practical tips. I've had John speak at my Mega Book Marketing events, and usually 100 percent of the attendees buy his book.

1001 Ways to Market Your Book covers selling to schools and libraries (libraries buy almost $2 billion in books every year), how to promote your book on the radio, how to get your book on best-seller lists, how to maximize subsidiary rights as an income stream, and several creative methods for getting people interested in your book online.

When you buy this book, don't feel overwhelmed by the page count. Decide to read ten pages each morning to inspire you for the book business. Make notes on ideas that stand out to you, and put them into action. There are so many available options that you really cannot go wrong with any one idea. If one doesn't work, simply move on to the next.

Part of being an author is discovering who you are in the midst of your work. You might find out you really enjoy talking on morning radio shows because you can do it while sitting in bed and sipping a mug of hot coffee. Or you'll discover you are a champion at marketing your book online, or perhaps it is promoting your book in person at live events that really turns you on. Whatever your preference turns out to be, make your business work for you rather working for your business.

Speak!

Every author has to learn how to speak and do to it well. My approach to speaking is unique. Toastmasters International, for instance, is a long-running organization that's been helpful to many people. But Toastmasters advises, "Write a great speech and then book a speaking engagement." I say, "Book the speaking engagement first and then figure out what you're going to say."

Admiral William H. McRaven is a perfect example. He gave a speech called "Make Your Own Bed." It was fun to read and think about. It became popular as a best-selling little book. Many parents gave it as gifts to their millennials. It worked so well that he is now chancellor of the University of Texas system.

Stay up late, get up early, and practice every paragraph on your friends. Keep this up until it's time for your presentation. You will be amazed how fast and efficiently your mind will start working. Do this whether you'll be speaking to five people at a small bookstore or to an audience of 3,000. Either way, be aware that you've got to show up and deliver a talk. For me, the secret is to come up with three key points and then link them together to deliver a grand slam home run. Please check my website for my audio products on mastering the fine art of speaking and prospering on the platform.

Use Bypass Marketing

Bypass marketing is a way of reaching the consumer outside the traditional channels of advertising and sales. The good news: bypass marketing is low-cost or no cost.

The challenge: it's do-it-yourself. Bypass marketing means coming up with novel ways of getting your product into the hands of people who can buy that product. You do that by thinking of win-win solutions that benefit everybody.

Go into restaurants and talk to the owners. Pitch the idea of making the book available to customers who are waiting to be seated, or even to read while eating if they happen to be alone. If the customer decides to purchase the book, the restaurant gets a percentage. It's win-win. There's no reason the restaurant shouldn't go for it.

We partnered with Dave Anderson, founder and owner of Famous Dave's BBQ. He gave our book out to everyone who came into his restaurants alone. They read it and usually cried. People at neighboring tables would come over to console the reader; they would take the book, read it, and also cry. Great new friendships were created. Each customer bought a book before leaving.

Dave loved it. It takes fourteen items to make a table ready (such as knives, forks, and napkins). The average bill at his chain is $13 with a $2 tip. Our book sold for $13. He earned $6, had no cleanup, the customer was emotionally wowed, his staff exuberantly happy, and the diners came back to eat there again. It was a superb win-win.

Think of situations in which you have a captive—places where it's easy to get people's attention because there's not a lot of distraction and their defenses are down. Beauty salons worked for us, as did chiropractor's offices. Plane flights are also a great opportunity. Every airline provides passengers with access to audio programming of one kind or another. Generally, it's just different genres of music, but there's also an opportunity to do a presentation from your book on airline audio. You can start with small feeder airlines and then bounce up to the larger carriers. My friend Scott Gross, who wrote *Positively Outrageous Customer Service*, came up with an outrageous and outstanding idea for Southwest Airlines. For one month, flight attendants announced they would send a roll of toilet paper down the center aisle of the airplane. The passenger who came closest to guessing the number of squares on the roll won a free copy of Scott's book. The book became a best seller in a month because of one very creative and well-executed idea.

On the topic of airlines, in-flight magazines are also important. It's not just a matter of getting an immediate sale. It's creating awareness of who you are and what you've written. If a passenger sees your name in an airline magazine and then sees your book in the airport bookstore, you're much more likely to get a sale at step 2 than if step 1 had never occurred. That's the power of bypass marketing. The more you do it, the more likely it is to benefit you. So tonight, drift off to sleep visualizing innovative ways to sell your book.

Find a Mentor

If you really want to see your gifts expand, you need to find a mentor. This should be someone you love, admire, and respect, someone who can help you move ahead on your path, and even teach you to see life in new and deeper ways. Every sports star has a coach: Michael Jordan had Phil Jackson. Every actor needs a director: Tom Hanks had Steven Spielberg. The musical production of *We Are the World* had twenty-eight superstars, who could only have worked together under the direction of the famous conductor Quincy Jones. Coaches, directors, and orchestra conductors have been inspiring mentors for countless creative and successful people. Trust me: you need a mentor too.

I was fortunate to have Dr. R. Buckminster Fuller, the Leonardo da Vinci of our era, as a mentor. Bucky, as he was affectionately called, took me under his wing and expanded who I am as a person. He got me to think comprehensively and synergistically, starting on the scale of the whole universe and then coming back to the specifics of everyday life. He convinced me that we could "make the world work for 100 percent of humanity, and that everyone can become physically and economically successful."

A mentor sees who you are, recognizes your beauty, inspires you, and empowers your message to bloom in the world. A mentor should not be concerned with making sure that you have enough to eat or have a roof over your head. They are in your life solely to guide your work, your destiny, and your service in the world. As Dr. Martin Luther King Jr. said, "We can all be great, because we can all serve greatly."

You might think it's an imposition to reach out to a more accomplished individual, but most successful people truly want to share what they have learned with someone who wants to learn it. Think of Yoda and Luke Skywalker. Skywalker needs to learn what Yoda has to teach in order to achieve his goal. But without Skywalker, what Yoda has to teach will be lost with him in the bog. The mentor-student relationship is a win-win. So don't be shy about approaching someone you respect, love, trust, and admire.

You might have to try out a few different people before you find the right match. It doesn't have to be someone famous. You might find a great mentor in a teacher at your local community college, a businessperson in your field, or the author of a book on your favorite subject.

A mentor will want to know that you value what is being shared with you. You are their legacy. You give them reflected glory. Their gift is living on in you. Do not be shy about initiating a mentor relationship if you feel called to do so. Be humble and helpful, and ask first what you can do to serve. You will be grateful you did.

When I was bankrupt and upside down in 1973–74, I had fortuitously sold my way through college and was given a prize of an audio recording by the dean of speakers, Cavett Robert. When I got it I was to sophomoric to drink in its vital and life changing wisdom. After being devastated by my bankruptcy, I listened to that one audio, *Are You The Cause Or Are You The Effect*, 287 times, making a check mark on the cassette every time I completed listening to it entirely. Courageously and innocently, I wrote this speaking giant and told him that when he arrived in New York, New Jersey, Connecticut, or Massachusetts, I would happily retrieve him and take him to his destination. Amazingly, he wrote back and told me when and where to pick him up.

I was broke, not poor, and I had a dilapidated Volkswagen. I retrieved Cavett and asked him everything I could think of about writing and speaking. He was beyond kind, gracious, insightful, and encouraging to me. I learned the profession of speaking and selling successfully from the platform thanks exclusively to Cavett, who also mentored Zig Ziglar and thousands of professional speakers.

Note that I did not know him when I wrote him. He had absolutely no obligation to mentor me. I am his reflected glory and thank him constantly for serving me. Now with my books and seminars, I have inspiringly touched over a billion people, with a desire to do infinitely more. You want a great and inspiring mentor. Somewhere there is someone who will serve you, so you can expandingly serve others.

Create BIG Events

Just because you don't have a book yet doesn't mean you can't speak on a stage, or create a BIG event. How? For one thing, you can always piggyback with a bigger name. Invite celebrities to be on your stage, or create an event that has meaning for a large number of men and women. Just make sure you are one of the big event's speakers. For example, if your book is about being a powerful woman, you might have an event for women about discovering their power and invite Oprah to speak.

Will she agree? You won't know until you ask. It's happened for lots of others, and it can happen for you too.

Big names usually want big money for live events, but don't be put off by that. Generally the money a person asks is an indication of their value. Just make sure you leverage the databases of your speakers. If your speaker has a database of 10,000 people, market your event to them, and you have your audience. They get to see their favorite speaker—and they also get to meet you. Peter Lowe built his giant seminar business by hiring Zig Ziglar. Lowe went on to invite big names like Bill Clinton, Colin Powell, Magic Johnson, and many more. This formula works.

Here's a great question to ask yourself when preparing a live event: "How little can I do and still be successful?" You see, a big name and a big topic don't necessarily mean a big audience. If the audience is willing to pay more for a ticket, you can limit the room size and the audience will feel a personal connection with the speaker. You'll make more without filling more seats.

Or you can joint-venture with a trade show. I joint-ventured with Reed Expositions, the host of Book Expo America. There were four best-selling authors and me. We attracted 850 attendees at $995 each, and after expenses, we split our profits 50-50.

I haven't said anything yet about free events, but don't overlook these. If you offer a complimentary event, just market something from the stage after you finish delivering tons of value to the audience. You can sell another well-priced event, a workshop, your book, a webinar, a telecourse, or anything else you can create.

Alex Mandossian, a very successful and well-respected Internet marketer who will soon be the first stay-at-home billionaire, likes to say, "Your book is actually your business card." So you can give away your book at a free event just as a gift. Then you should also offer a weeklong retreat, a weekend seminar, or even a twelve-week telecourse (which you can teach while sitting on your couch in your pajamas!).

Whatever freebie you choose, there is good money in events that can give you exposure for yourself and your book. Getting up on a stage—any stage—means you are an expert in your field.

The master of giving away free books to get audience and make millions and millions is Dean Graziosi. Dean is a serial entrepreneur, infomercial king, and author of many books like *Secrets of the Millionaires*. I did a very successful and vastly profitable infomercial with Dean, so I know he is a talented and renowned visionary.

Most recently, his mastermind creatively partnered with Tony Robbins and entrepreneur Russell Brunson created the KBB (Knowledge Broker Blueprint) and sold the most product ever sold at one time in our industry to prove impact. They made the most outrageous offer ever and, it is reported, took in $42 million in a weekend, it is reported online. It took over a year and the creativity of many superstars in our industry to bring this to fruition. Purportedly, they will be repeating their event.

This example proves what I am suggesting above. Creativity, innovation, branding, and big-name messengers can make a relatively instant impact. You can view the KBB blueprint online for free. There is no reason you can't do something similar or even more epic, if you work at it tirelessly and inventively. The best is yet to be.

Take Pictures Everywhere

When you write a book, you're asking people to pay attention to you. Why should they do that? Everybody has too much to think about already. Why should they think about you? The answer is simple. You've got to make yourself more interesting than all the other stuff (that is, the marketplace noise) that's out there. You've got to create yourself as a larger-than-life personality. It's a matter of magnifying your life experiences, first in your own eyes and then in everyone else's.

That's why I'm constantly taking pictures of the people I meet and the places I visit. It's a way of saying, "This is interesting! This is exciting! This is fun! This is worth a picture!" And that's really the way I feel. If I don't feel that way, why do I think anybody is going to read something I've written? I want to invite people into my life and into my world. A really easy way for them to enter my world is to be in a photo with me, or to see the photos I've taken. They're on the Internet at www.smugmug.com. Search "Mark Victor Hansen" for over 17,000 pictures of me.

My photos there are everywhere, or at least I'd like them to be. It's not about ego. It's not because I think I'm beautiful. It's because exciting and entertaining things are happening for me, and I want you, my readers, to be part of that. Do the same thing (or more!) for your readers.

Dexter Yeager was the biggest of the big distributors in Amway and held gargantuan rallies around the country. Along with President George H. W. Bush, singer LeAnn Rimes, author Doug Wead, and many celebrities and leaders, I was hired to talk to 38,000 distributors. After I talked, I stood in line for twelve and a half hours signing books and taking pictures. When finished, I was exhausted.

Jim Rohn told me that when I went to Asia, an audience of 104,000 would show up for pictures. In China, where I sold 374 million books, I frequently had 12,000 people in an audience. My promoter limited the picture taking by charging $500 for a photo with Crystal and me. It was amazing and humbling to see the throngs of folks who wanted a picture with us.

Get on Magazine Covers

I've been on the cover of a lot of magazines—like *Success* and *Time*—and I've sold a lot of books. My books have made it onto the front pages of *The Los Angeles Times, The New York Times,* and other major papers around the globe. I know what you're thinking: "Mark, don't I have to be famous to get on a magazine's cover?" The answer is no. So how can you make it happen?

Start by finding publications that serve your niche market. Suppose you're an astrologer who has written a book for teenagers. Do you think you will have an easier time getting on the cover of *People* or on the cover of a magazine that specializes in astrology? So first target magazines that serve your future buyers. Ask for a cover story. Tell the magazine's editor exactly why you would be a compelling person to choose. What about you or your story is so extraordinary that their readers will connect to you?

Magazines choose their covers based on sales potential. So when you speak with editors, explain why a cover story about you will sell more copies of their publication. You don't have to be that blunt about it, but you do want to capture their attention in a way that makes them think, "If I feature this person, my readers will love him or her, and we can pick up some new readership as well."

Once you get your book written, get it in the news! If it's just the front page of your small community newspaper, that's great! You can send that paper to the magazine whose cover you're hoping to get on. When editors see you in print, it is much easier to see you as their cover story. Local magazines and newspapers are always looking for interesting people to write about, so get out there and make the news!

During the O. J. Simpson murder trial, jury members were not allowed to read newspapers, watch TV, or listen to any news reports. However, they could read books. For Jack and me, it was a perfect opportunity to shine. We sent *Chicken Soup for the Soul* books to Judge Lance Ito and, with his permission, all the jurors. Each and every day, they proudly carried our books into court, and *Chicken Soup* became a real news item. Later, when two jurors were interviewed, they said the only good thing about being sequestered was reading our books.

The point is, watch the news and use it innovatively to your advantage. Read the news with an eye and mindset for becoming a positive and illuminating part of it.

By the way, the flip side of your success in getting on magazine covers is maintaining great relationships with the editors who featured you. Send flowers to thank them for your covers. Make sure they remember you as someone easy to work with and someone who appreciated them. That will set the stage for future features on you and your books.

You should also maintain a relationship with the photographers who shot your pictures. These photographers are often freelancers, meaning they probably photograph the covers of many different magazines. If would be nice if your name were on their minds when they hear of other publications looking for a cover story.

Create Partnerships and Affiliates

My friend Rick Dearr is an Internet marketing expert and the author of three best-selling books. Rick's description of affiliate marketing is clear and to the point: "'Affiliate' is just another word for 'commissioned salesperson.'" If you had a computer store and employed someone to go out and sell computers to businesses, you might pay them a commission. An army of affiliates is the same thing.

As a marketer, you may worry about people you perceive as competitors. You may think those people can't be of help to you, but the truth is, you should reach out to everyone! Those you see as competitors could turn out to be very good friends. After all, they're in the same market as you. They understand what you're going through because they're trying to do the same things. You may find that the market is big enough for both of you, or even a dozen of you. So don't worry about your market being so competitive that you can't approach everyone. True, some people will feel that you're their competition and won't want to help. That's OK. But others will see the big picture. They're going to help you because they're going to benefit as well.

The basic idea of affiliate marketing is this: you partner with a trusted source who then campaigns for you in exchange for a percentage of profit (15–20 percent is standard).

For example, suppose you have a pizza business and you create an affiliate relationship with a rental store across the street. With that relationship, you can drive business to each other. It can be two-way or one-way traffic. You might put a coupon for movies on your pizza boxes, or you might offer them a percentage of whatever business they bring you. There are several ways to structure the relationship, but the idea is the same. Your customers trust you and rely on your services, so what and who you recommend to them is coming from someone they trust.

Let's say you have a friend who writes a weekly email to her database of 10,000 people. You might ask her to write a review of your book. Then you create a code for her, so that anyone who buys your book types her promotion code, and she gets 20 percent of that sale.

Affiliate marketing really motivates people to get behind you, especially if they believe in your message and think they can make money by helping you. The key here is to be generous enough so that they will stay motivated. It will not serve you to be cheap with your affiliates. They are basically gifting you with word-of-mouth marketing, which, in spite of zillion-dollar ad campaigns, is still the most powerful form of marketing out there.

Find a Pitch Partner

Most writers do not speak about their work easily. In the movie business, it is the producer's job to pitch the writer's work or idea to a production company or network, not the writer's. The writer usually attends the pitch meeting but does not say much. Why? Writers, by nature, are mostly introverts. (Zig Ziglar, an introvert, claimed that he trained himself to become an extrovert on stage only.) They do not summon much of the natural enthusiasm that comes so easily for extroverts.

If that sounds like you, you need to find a pitch partner. (In a perfect world, this person is *not* your mother.) Your pitch partner is someone who loves your book and raves about you. Now it the time to throw your arm around that person and say, "Hey, how would you like to talk to so-and-so for me?" And you make it worth their while to get out there and toot your horn.

Your pitch partner might be present at meetings with you, throw you a party, or write about you on their Facebook pages or the myriad of social media. They can also take you to social mixers where they will introduce you and your work to people that need to know who you are because they could, in some way, advance your career.

The key is to find someone for whom this comes completely naturally. They already love your work, are motivated to let the world know how brilliant you are, and possess some skills at making—and maintaining—connections. You don't want a pitch partner who insists they are the most excellent networker in town, but have zero names in their database, or were tossed out of the last three parties they attended.

You want a pitch partner who enhances your reputation, not diminishes it. If it is someone other than your best friend, you will want to create a simple contract that states exactly what he or she gains by doing this extra work for you. Obviously there is a fine line between the friend who just wants to help you out by sending out a quick email to their friends about you and who never does anything more, and a *real* pitch partner, who makes introductions or deals that put money in your pocket by doing the talking for you. If you're not sure what kind of compensation is appropriate, ask them what they want, and see if that sounds reasonable to you.

If you are going to a very important meeting to talk about your work or career and you have your pitch partner in place, the next step is to videotape a mock meeting. You can even have a friend or family member stand in for the person to whom you are pitching the book. Record what your pitch partner says, then play it back and critique it together. A production executive at Paramount Studios used this technique in his office, bringing in his staff and making them all practice pitches together so that they were ready for their big network meetings, in which millions of dollars were on the table. He took his writers and their work seriously, and so should you.

Another way to enroll a pitch partner is pitch to someone important and advance their businesses or protocols. Recently we met and befriended serial entrepreneur Jeff Hoffman, the serial entrepreneur (I have encouraged you to watch him avidly online and be wowed). Jeff wants to inspire "self-determination to entrepreneurship." I want to help Jeff do that and have actively pitched him to many dynamite podcasts that we have been on.

It is a big win for Jeff, because I am a free publicist, so to speak. It's great for a podcaster who wants brilliantly successful giants on his show. It's great for me because it keeps me at the front of the mind for Jeff and his vastly interesting and growing enterprises, in which we can potentially participate.

Make the Call!

The telephone is such an interesting piece of technology. For some reason, it's frightening to many people, which leads to some very negative effects. Surveys show that more business is lost because of a client's negative experience on the telephone than for any other reason.

Everyone has a love-hate relationship with the phone, yet there are more people talking on the phone than ever before in history. A lot more. It's estimated that 8 billion smartphones are now in circulation around the world. With 5G, which will offer the Internet of things, (the IOT), it will include virtually everyone over eighteen years old.

In the book business, as in any commercial enterprise, you've got to be confident in your telephone skills—especially since so many people aren't.

Beyond people's love-hate relationship with their phones, there's also a huge amount of fear. Why? It's the fear of rejection, which, as we've discussed, is a very deep-seated emotion. But suppose the possibility of rejection could be entirely removed. I give you absolute permission to believe that henceforward, you are rejection-proof. Now make the calls with courage, calm confidence, and resolute self-assurance that you will be listened to, respected, and supported.

Suppose you could just punch in a number and know that whoever answers will be thrilled to hear from you. There's no shortcut to making that happen, but it involves many of the same elements that go into becoming a best-selling author.

Pay attention to the basics. Be interested in people, and they'll be interested in you. Think about what you can offer them. What can you provide that they really want? Answer that question, and people will definitely take you up on your offer. Why wouldn't they? *But first they must know who you are.* If you've done the work described here in part 2, you'll never be treated like a stranger.

Use the Four D's to Create Focus

When there's something that needs your attention, you have four choices: you can dump it, delegate it, defer it, or do it. I call them the four D's.

Dump it is probably the most important one to learn. This has been tough for me. When you have a certain amount of success, you'll find that you'll get all kinds of offers. You must learn how to say no. You can choose to say yes, but you must always remember that you have the ability to say no. Only then can you really focus on the things you want and need to do.

Either delegate or stagnate. ***Delegate*** a task to someone competent and desirous of doing an excellent job. I could do accounting, but I don't like it, am not efficient at it, and have experts who love crunching my numbers, so I delegate this task to them.

Defer it. It you defer a task that must be done, give yourself a calendar reminder to complete it on this day at this time.

Parkinson's law suggests that work expands or contracts based on the time you have available for it. When a publisher mandated a delivery of a book that Jack and I had contracted to do, but had no time or interest in, we had to use Parkinson's law. I quickly and effectively interviewed 101 individuals. I pulled out their brilliance, wisdom, and insights and collated them into a semblance of exciting readability, and Jack did a quick edit.

We accomplished a miracle. The book was *The Aladdin Factor* and sold 3.6 million copies.

Parkinson's law dominated our minds, brains, and souls, and that one month contracted so that we could make a superb product in a relatively impossible time frame.

Do it. "Just Do It!" It's the Nike slogan. Once you make a real and solid decision, Once you are all in, once you are in tune with the infinite, and once you have thought through all it will take to write your book, just do it. When Sylvester Stallone, then a B actor, got the idea for *Rocky,* the story is that he locked himself into a quiet space and wrote the script in three and a half days. He then demanded that he play the role. That launched sequels and prequels, put him on the A-list, and earned him multiple millions.

When you read *Chicken Soup for the Writer's Soul*, you will see that every writer ultimately faces the challenge of Parkinson's law for a multiplicity of reasons and has to just DO IT!

PART THREE

Missed Fortune: A Sample Proposal

The following is an extremely effective proposal for the mainstream publication of a book that has already been self-published by the author. Notice the professionalism with which the book's publishing history is described. Notice also that the author's effectiveness as a marketer for the book is prominently featured. This is clearly a business proposal, which is exactly as it should be. Many thanks to the great literary agent Jillian Manus for sharing this most useful document!

Missed Fortune

Dispel the Money-Myth Conceptions:
Isn't It Time You *Became Wealthy?*

Editions

First Test Edition Indicates Potential

In June 2002, the author self-published 500 copies of his book for test marketing. He sold all 500 within 90 days. With each copy, he included an evaluation questionnaire. Over 100 people returned evaluations, all with overwhelmingly positive responses. (Qualitative results can be shared upon request.)

Above all, responders appreciated the book's details, which backed up the financial strategies, even though some readers merely skimmed the examples and numbers. Many readers reread the book two and three times, stating they would use it as a valuable reference for years to come.

The author also sent 40 copies of the book randomly to existing clients for their critique. Not only was feedback positive, but as a direct result of clients reeducating themselves on these strategies, his firm, Paramount Financial Services, Inc., generated over $500,000 of new revenue with these clients' subsequent activity.

Second Test Edition Yields Results

The author made about 2,000 grammatical changes to the second test edition and printed 1,000 copies. No general advertising was done to promote the book. He introduced it at two insurance industry trade shows; about 100 books were sold at each. From there, word of mouth spread across the country, and our supply was drained within four months. We had to run an emergency reprint of the second test edition before the next edit was complete.

Over the past six months, this book also has been introduced at 8 conferences and seminars. The audiences averaged about 50 attendees with an average of 60 books placed at each event, purchased for distribution to their friends or associates.

Another promising outlet is the nationwide network of financial advisors the author founded, called The Equity Enhancement Matrix (TEEM). In order to become a TEEM member, a financial professional pays a tuition of $3,500 for a three-day intensive training in Salt Lake City, Utah. There prospective members observe the author's seminars to the general public and learn how to prepare the book's plans and implement its strategies for their clients. The TEEM members have commented that this experience is the best $3,500 they have invested in their careers. Each TEEM member receives 40 copies of the book to help them get started. In various market tests, they have found that for every 40 books placed in the hands of their clients and prospects, a minimum of $100,000 of new revenue is generated within the following 90 days. They show TEEM members how to conduct at least one seminar per month, where at least 40–50 books are placed, likewise resulting in a dramatic return on their investment. (TEEM members purchase books at 40 percent off retail in bulk quantities of 40–100 books per order.)

They also have test-marketed the book with mortgage companies and brokers. When they have loaned a copy of the book to customers obtaining a new mortgage or refinancing, over 50 percent come back a week later to apply for the mortgage and request to purchase the book. They also increase the amount of their mortgage by an average of 40 percent as a result of the education this book offers. This subsequently increases the revenue earned per mortgage for the mortgage broker. After interest rates begin to rise again, mortgage companies will be clamoring for ways to generate new mortgage volume. This book provides an incredible and proven solution for them.

Third Test Edition in Demand

A third revised test edition, with about 500 minor improvements, was published in April, and 1,000 books were sold within 60 days by word of mouth only.

First Official Edition Enclosed

The author has just released the official first edition, which was printed on June 20. The book is also being divided into a series of four smaller books, which can be purchased separately or together in a jacketed sleeve. The titles of the individual books belonging to the *Missed Fortune* series will likely be: *Homemade Wealth, IRA/401(k) and Other Money Traps, Wealth Enhancement Strategies,* and *Wealth Empowerment.*

Seminars

The author has developed a seminar and has conducted it successfully for the past ten years. Until last year, it was titled "Common Sense Strategies for Successful Equity Management." His book was written as a result of his seminar's success. He needed to reach more people, so in writing his book, he took this approach: "If I had 20 hours of someone's undivided attention, what would I say and in what order would I say it?" Last year he renamed the seminar to coincide with the title of the book. The book has greatly enhanced the appeal to the attendee, who now can purchase a copy and study the concepts in more depth. Attendees comment that they do not feel at all pressured to buy the book, yet an average of 83 percent and as many as 100 percent have purchased books following each seminar. The author conducts about 12 seminars a year in Utah using full-page ads such as the one enclosed.

Colleges and Universities

The author is currently working with 46 colleges and universities throughout the country, and the list is growing monthly. He is initially asked to speak to smaller groups composed of college presidents, development directors, and investment committee chairs. He gives them a complimentary copy of his book.

Two marketing opportunities are emerging. The development offices are organizing groups of their high net worth alumni who have expressed a desire to give substantial gifts to the college or university but have not yet done so. In fact, only 6 percent end up giving because: (1) they don't know how; (2) they don't want to disinherit their children; or (3) they don't want to kill the goose laying the golden eggs for their family wealth. Through the strategies he teaches in section 4 of his book, the author helps affluent families empower their wealth and give without giving up anything. Hence he is invited to be the keynote speaker at alumni banquets and special occasions.

The second opportunity exists in the business and finance departments. They are asking for adjunct reading material for their finance classes that teach methods and views opposing those usually found in traditional money management books. A list of the colleges and universities that he is working with are attached.

Speaking Engagements

The author is currently involved in about four speaking engagements per month at conferences, symposiums, workshops, and conventions. He has been speaking to select audiences of anywhere from 50 to 2,000. However, because of time and scheduling constraints, he is now forced to be more selective in selecting speaking opportunities. He just spoke at the Million Dollar Round Table in Las Vegas on June 23, 2003. The room was set up for 1,000 attendees. The doorkeepers let in 1,300 until there was standing room only. They say they turned away another 300 because of fire code restrictions. Hence the author knows the subject matter is of great interest to those desiring to attend; they sold 1,090 books the following three days as a result. He was only able to sign about 250 of them. He believes the ratios would be similar if the attendance was 10,000. The Million Dollar Round Table Power Center (bookstore), Amazon.com, and the author continue to sell copies daily since the convention. He knows he can direct a lot of sales to bookstores following each speaking engagement.

Talk Shows

The author has participated in several talk shows on various topics. He has had extensive training in radio speaking and oratory in college, so he feels very comfortable speaking on the air. He believes there will be more promotional opportunities than he has capacity to handle, so again he will need to be selective in accepting them. There is a high demand for authors who have written books that contain unorthodox approaches to accumulating wealth. His proven financial strategies take the opposite approach to the usual view of paying off a home and suggest why it may not be wise to participate in a 401(k). Radio talk show hosts love controversial subjects with new insights.

Conventions and Trade Shows

The author is very comfortable speaking in almost any setting where the audience comes for education and enlightenment. He gives a popular, high-energy, 60-minute presentation titled, "Ten Keys to Achieving a Meaningful Transformation to [the organization's top sales level] and Beyond!" He can adapt this talk to any sales organization relying upon sales, from cosmetics to insurance. No matter what the audience demographics are, attendees buy the book afterward.

In the last 120 days, the author has spoken at Amelia Island, Florida; Raleigh, North Carolina; Knoxville, Tennessee; Chicago; Las Vegas; Honolulu; Philadelphia; Scottsdale, Arizona; Salt Lake City, Utah; San Diego; and Los Angeles. During the next 90 days, he has speaking engagements scheduled in Raleigh; Charlotte, North Carolina; Knoxville; Nashville; Chicago; Kansas City; Las Vegas; Los Angeles; Salt Lake City; Honolulu; Rancho Mirage, California; and 17 colleges and universities spread between California and Florida.

Simple and Easy to Understand

People comment that the author has a unique ability to take complex financial issues and make them simple and easy to understand. Readers will find the book easy reading, because they learn through interesting examples, case studies, and illustrations. It contains plenty of technical details—again, explained simply—that will educate and enlighten everyone from the novice to the expert. Purchasers of *Missed Fortune* comment that it was highly recommended to them by sharp, intelligent people they respect. If the book was loaned to them by a friend, they call because they want to purchase a copy for their own library. Many readers say they have read the book through two or three times within a month. They often go to their financial advisors with the book heavily highlighted and dog-eared.

Missed Fortune takes a more step-by-step approach to wealth accumulation. It details actual strategies and dot-to-dot methods on how to methodically take two assets (home equity and retirement savings) and strategically reposition them to dramatically enhance net worth over time.

Sequels and Future Publications

Three short chapters at the end of the book in section 4 purposely set the stage for three or four sequels to *Missed Fortune* on topics such as IRA and 401(k) retirement planning; empowering wealth; teaching children how to fish rather than throwing them fish; strategies for charitable giving; and a more detailed dot-to-dot workbook on managing equity in real estate. The author believes that all have incredible potential.

Strategic Alliances

The author is creating a very strong market with his strategic alliances. All of the TEEM members who invest $3,500 to learn his system will spread the message about this book, which will generate tremendous demand at bookstores. His goal is to have 1,000 certified TEEM members teaching his seminar nationwide within the next 18 months.

Several banks and insurance companies are beginning to use this book with their customer base.

Four national mortgage companies—Kendall Todd, Mortgage Tree Lending, World Lending Group, and Mortgage Superstars—are beginning to use his book to increase their mortgage volume by 40 percent without increasing the number of loans they process. His book provides solutions to maintain a thriving mortgage business when interest rates go back up (and they will). Just today, they sent invitations to 385 mortgage brokers in the Salt Lake City area for three seminars he is conducting next week. A complimentary copy of the book is given to them. Those that catch the vision purchase 40 copies of the book to begin lending to their mortgage customers. Those same mortgage customers purchase a copy for their own library 60 percent of the time.

Several other strategic alliances are also promoting the book as they conduct their businesses because of the enhancement provided by *Missed Fortune.*

Retail and Wholesale Pricing Options

1. Publish the work as one book under the title of *Missed Fortune: Dispel the Money Myth-Conceptions: Isn't It Time* You *Became Wealthy?* Hardbound retail price, $34.97; paperback retail price, $24.97.

2. Separate the book into four smaller books priced as follows:

	Electronic Copies	Paperback Copies
Preface, Introduction, Table of Contents	FREE	N/A
Book 1: Homemade Wealth	$8.00	$9.97
Book 2: IRA/401(k) and Other Money Traps	$6.00	$7.50
Book 3: Wealth Enhancement Strategies	$12.00	$14.97
Book 4: Wealth Empowerment	$4.00	$4.97
Total:	$30.00	$37.41

A 20 percent discount is offered when the entire series is purchased at once at $24 for electronic copies, $29.97 for paperback copies.

Comparative Survey

***Rich Dad Poor Dad*, by Robert T. Kiyosaki**

Missed Fortune takes a more step-by-step approach to wealth accumulation than *Rich Dad Poor Dad. Missed Fortune* details actual strategies and dot-to-dot methods for methodically taking two assets (home equity and retirement savings) and strategically repositioning them to dramatically enhance net worth over time. College finance professors who have been recommending *Rich Dad Poor Dad* as supplemental reading material have been asking for books with more meat on exactly how to enhance net worth rather than books simply about money. *Missed Fortune* satisfies that appetite.

The Millionaire Next Door, by Thomas J. Stanley and William D. Danko

Missed Fortune does not focus on the habits and character traits of millionaires. Rather it focuses on 23 common myths about money and wealth accumulation. Many concepts in *Missed Fortune* oppose what the common millionaire (next door) believes. Instead it teaches concepts practiced by megamillionaires and shows how a common homeowner can implement these same strategies on a smaller scale to achieve a multimillion-dollar net worth. *Missed Fortune* shows how to do things *differently* to dramatically enhance one's net worth.

The Road to Wealth, by Suze Orman

Suze's book is a great reference guide to the common approach to accumulating money, whereas *Missed Fortune* takes an unorthodox approach—examining such things as how to pay off your home by keeping it mortgaged to the hilt, and why participation in an IRA or 401(k) plan is not always the best retirement savings option. The author directly opposes Suze's recommendations on the proper use of life insurance. *Missed Fortune* goes into far greater depth, providing actual numerical proof that will challenge the typical recommendations not only of Suze Orman but of many other financial advisors. This book is not for financial jellyfish who need to have their hands held, but for disciplined savers and investors.

The One Minute Millionaire,
by Mark Victor Hansen and Robert G. Allen

The One Minute Millionaire is an excellent work and most closely resembles the philosophies and strategies contained in *Missed Fortune.*

The authors are personal friends of the author, who enjoys their association in their Millionaires Summit. They have reviewed this book and think it has remarkable potential. The author will get endorsements from them.

Missed Fortune is different in that it zeroes in on specific assets that the common homeowner or wage earner can begin to better manage to become a millionaire without increasing their outlay by one dime. *Missed Fortune* focuses on 23 common misconceptions about money and explain the realities. It then gives a wealth enhancement strategy in each chapter and goes on to prove numerically how it works and how to do it. This is a less sensational approach—showing how to become a millionaire slowly, safely, and methodically.

The Ultimate Safe Money Guide by Martin D. Weiss

Missed Fortune challenges many of Dr. Weiss's philosophies and recommendations head-on. The author shows people, especially over age 50 (which is his target audience) how to choose profitable investments that are often in direct opposition to Weiss's. *Missed Fortune* will hopefully clear up misunderstandings regarding the insurance and brokerage industries that Dr. Weiss has labeled as scams. The author predicts that his book will be much better received as the ultimate safe money guide for people over age 50 because of his style of communication and use of inoffensive language.

PART FOUR

The One Minute Millionaire: A Marketing Plan

Here is the marketing plan Robert Allen and I developed for our very successful book, *The One Minute Millionaire*. In writing this plan, we were very aware that great things begin with great goals. We said to ourselves, "Let's begin with the end in mind."

Marketing Plan for *The One Minute Millionaire*

A major new blockbuster by *New York Times* number 1 best-selling authors Mark Victor Hansen (MVH) and Robert G. Allen (RGA).

Publishing Objectives

1. *The One Minute Millionaire* (OMM) is the first book in history to become a *New York Times* number 1 best seller *simultaneously* on the *fiction* and *non-fiction* lists.
2. *The One Minute Millionaire* has prepaid orders for 1 million hardcover copies before publication date.
3. *The One Minute Millionaire* sells 10 million books in the first 36 months.
4. *The One Minute Millionaire* helps raise $10 million for related charities and causes.

Action Plan for *The One Minute Millionaire*

For a book to be hugely successful, it needs the right title at the right time and must be backed by an ingenious and coordinated marketing and promotional strategy. We're sure that you, as a publisher with a sizable investment in this book, want to know how we, the authors, will support and enhance the sale of this book. Following you will find our 28-point marketing plan to reach the audacious goals we have listed at the top of this page.

1. We understand the importance of aggressive marketing and promotion.

Most authors have no idea how to sell books. They leave the marketing and selling up to the publisher, cross their fingers, and hope that the book catches on.

Neither of us is that kind of author!

We realize that the author and the publisher have to work together as a powerful team with an aggressive plan to create maximum exposure for the book. Our previous best sellers did not happen by accident. Neither will this one.

2. As active public speakers, we will introduce OMM to our audiences.

For the past twenty years, both MVH and RGA have spoken at least 5 times a month to various audiences worldwide. We estimate that before *OMM*'s publication date, we will have collectively spoken to at least 150,000–200,000 people in live audiences. Each person will be encouraged to purchase the book for gifts, holidays, and special occasions. We'll either give them special discount coupons or presell the book on the spot.

We believe that we can deliver a minimum of 25,000 advance paid orders for the book just from this vehicle alone.

Why are we so confident? Because we've already done it. With the release of volume 1 of *Chicken Soup for the*

Soul in 1994, MVH delivered 25,000 advance sales from his speaking engagements. With the April 2000 release of *Multiple Streams of Income*, RGA delivered 10,000 advance and post-pub-date sales. Because of this experience, we feel confident in our ability to generate an *additional 75,000 paid orders* through our speaking engagements in the three years following the publication of OMM.

3. We both have huge databases of satisfied customers who already want this book.

MVH delivers over 875,000 Chicken Soup for the Soul stories DAILY via email through the Chicken Soup website. Many of these readers are women who will welcome the story of a woman heroine who overcomes great odds to earn a million dollars. MVH will incorporate a link at the bottom of each of these emails, driving interested people to the OMM website. In addition to his email list, MVH maintains an in-house mailing list of 40,000 loyal customers.

RGA has been teaching financial freedom for over 20 years. Three million people have attended his free evening investment seminars. Another 103,000 people have attended his $500 weekend investment seminars, while 20,000 people have attended his $5,000 week-long Wealth Training. At present 2,000 people are currently enrolled in his $4,000 Protégé program, and 60,000 people have purchased his $60 audiotape programs through

Nightingale/Conant. He maintains a current mailing list of over 100,000 of these satisfied customers. They are perfect buyers for this book.

In addition to these databases, MVH and RGA have access to hundreds of thousands of additional names from the databases of close associates and partners in other ventures. For example, 377,000 Americans have birthdays each and every day. We have access to this database and will plan a targeted promotion to this list.

We intend on using these resources to mount a direct mail campaign for the new book. We feel very confident we can generate the sale of at least 50,000 books from our direct mail efforts.

4. We will generate valuable exposure through newspaper and magazine columns.

Every Thursday, a Chicken Soup for the Soul column (syndicated with King Features) appears in over 165 newspapers (143 daily and 22 weekly) with a total readership of 17.5 million nationwide. This gives enormous exposure to the Chicken Soup series and generates thousands of sales. In addition, *Woman's World* weekly magazine (1.5 million readers) runs a syndicated Chicken Soup story.

Building on this experience, we intend to launch a nationwide financial column called "The Millionaire Minute." The tagline will drive people to the One Minute Millionaire website, where people will be encouraged to sign up for our free e-newsletter. In addition to building awareness of the book, it will also give us the opportunity to capture email addresses and send interested readers targeted messages about it.

5. We have two very successful websites that will help promote the sale of OMM.

We have registered the domain name www.oneminute millionaire.com and will have the site up and running well before the publication of the book. Linked to this new site will be the Chicken Soup for the Soul website (100,000 unique visitors a day plus 875,000 daily email subscribers, with a strategy to increase this number to 5 million in the next 18 months).

RGA also maintains a website at www.multiple streamsofincome.com. It sends out a regular email e-zine currently to 20,000 subscribers. By the end of 2000, the subscriber list will expand to 100,000, and by the end of 2001 the subscriber list will be over 250,000. Using targeted marketing, each of these subscribers will be given the opportunity to buy *The One Minute Millionaire* before publication day.

6. We will use the latest Internet marketing techniques to promote OMM.

Internet marketing is still in its infancy. Most websites lose money because they don't understand marketing.

RGA is currently writing a new book on Internet marketing based on the latest cutting-edge research. It will be released by Wiley in the spring of 2001. In researching the book, RGA conducted a live, documented test to see how much money could be generated in a targeted marketing challenge in 24 hours. RGA was able to make $94,532.44 in CASH in 24 hours with zero marketing dollars.

By the time OMM is released, we will be using sophisticated Internet marketing strategies with a goal of generating at least 100,000 Internet book sales in the first 12 months.

We have associations with other successful Internet ventures who have already agreed to promote this book to their customers. (For example, OneWorldLive.com is an extremely successful and profitable Internet portal with 1.3 million unique visitors per month. The managing director and co-owner is actress Melanie Griffith. MVH and RGA are content experts for the site and will be able to promote their new book on this site.) We will add dozens of other web partners before the publication date.

7. We will take advantage of our existing consulting relationships.

MVH is a top spokesperson with Enrich International, a rapidly expanding worldwide network of 750,000 distributors of herbal and vitamin products worldwide. Because of his high visibility, he has a unique advantage to be able to recommend certain books. One of the books he will recommend will be *The One Minute Millionaire.* It is a perfect book because the sales force is composed primarily of women, who are a prime target for this message of hope and inspiration.

RGA is a top spokesperson with USANA, Inc., a rapidly growing worldwide network of 200,000 distributors of vitamin and skincare products. Because of his high visibility, he has the same unique advantage as MVH—except in a different company. *The One Minute Millionaire* will be a hot seller among this database of motivation-hungry salespeople.

We feel that we can conservatively generate the sale of 20,000 books through these two companies. We can orchestrate the sales of these books to happen during a specific week in the launch of OMM so that the sales give maximum leverage for the best seller lists.

8. We will launch targeted promotional activities for this book.

Both MVH and RGA are masters at promotion.

In promoting *Chicken Soup for the Soul*, MVH was involved in dozens of major promotional activities. To name a few of the most exciting:

- Covers of the Chicken Soup books were affixed to 50 million cartons of Diet Coke for 6 months. Inside the cartons were free samplers of stories from *Chicken Soup for the Couple's Soul*, which has now sold over a million copies.

- Feed LA on Turkey Day: Chicken Soup authors helped feed real chicken soup to 10,000 homeless people at the Union Rescue Mission in Los Angeles during Thanksgiving.
- IAMS pet food bought tens of thousands of Chicken Soup books to help promote *Chicken Soup for the Pet Lover's Soul.* They spent $2 million on the promotion, which drove the book to number 1 in one week.
- The Red Cross gave free samples of *Chicken Soup* booklets to 1.5 million volunteer blood donors. This generated massive positive publicity. This helped sell over 3 million copies of *Chicken Soup III.*
- Campbell's Soup placed *Chicken Soup for the Soul* stories on 600 million cans of chicken soup.
- PAX TV airs *Chicken Soup for the Soul* every Tuesday and Sunday nights nationwide.
- The world's largest book signing in history occurred with *Chicken Soup for the Kid's Soul* on September 19, 1998. Book signings were simultaneously held in 129 cities in 29 states. This helped push the sale to 1.9 million books and several appearances at the number 1 spot.

Because of these and many other activities, the authors of *Chicken Soup* were listed in the *Guinness Book of World*

Records as having the most titles on the *New York Times* best-seller list simultaneously. On May 24, 1998, there were a total of seven Chicken Soup books on the list!

Robert Allen is also no stranger to promotion.

In promoting his first book, *Nothing Down*, he convinced Simon & Schuster to run full-page ads in major newspapers with the daring headline:

"Send me to any city. Take away my wallet. Give me $100 for living expenses, and in 72 hours, I'll buy an excellent piece of real estate using none of my own money."

The ad was enormously successful. It attracted the attention of the *Los Angeles Times,* who challenged him to live up to his claim. They flew him to San Francisco, where, with a reporter by his side, he proceeded to buy six properties worth more than $500,000—in just 57 hours.

The front page of the *LA Times* business section read:

"Buying Home without Cash: Investor Accepts *Times* Challenge and Wins."

The article was picked up by dozens of newspapers nationwide, generating instant attention and credibility and driving the book to the top of the best-seller lists.

Two years later, RGA followed up with an equally impressive challenge:

"Send me to any unemployment line, let me select someone who is out of work and discouraged. In two days, I'll

teach him the secrets of wealth, and in ninety days, he'll be back on his feet with $5,000 cash in the bank, never to set foot in an unemployment line again."

Once again, RGA delivered. He selected Mary Bonenberger, an unemployed housewife from St. Louis, Missouri (the "Show Me" State). Within ninety days, Mary had earned $5,000 cash and went on to buy several million dollars' worth of real estate. To celebrate, Robert took her on *Good Morning America* with him, generating even more publicity.

The story was carried in many national newspapers, with an obvious impact on book sales.

RGA has also fulfilled challenges made by the television media. Regis Philbin challenged to come on his show, pick someone from the audience at random, teach them for 90 days, and prove that they could make some serious money in a short period of time. He selected Pat Watson, from Brooklyn. Pat was an African-American woman working as a part-time schoolteacher. Her husband was a garbage collector. Under RGA's tutelage, she was able to make $20,000 in just 90 days and returned on the show to report her results. The audience was electrified. Regis loved it. His producer loved it. His audience loved it. On a similar show in San Francisco, the woman RGA picked from the studio audience made $50,000 in ninety days.

Because of this and other promotions, *Publishers Weekly* listed *Nothing Down* as the number 11 hardcover nonfiction best seller for the entire decade of the 1980s.

For *The One Minute Millionaire*, we propose to organize similar PR exposure—starting with the release of thousands of butterflies on the day is book is launched. Why butterflies? You'll have to read the book to find out.

9. We will launch radio and TV syndicated spots before the book appears.

Under the theme of The Millionaire Minute, the authors will produce one-minute segments for radio and TV on topics such as:

- How to make $1 million on as little as a dollar a day.
- How to think like a millionaire.
- How to buy your next home for 10–20 percent below market.
- Time is money: why disorganized people can't get rich.
- Your child, the future millionaire.
- And other timely financial topics.

The tagline will encourage people to visit the OneMinuteMillionaire.com website to learn more about financial success. Each visitor will enter their email address and will receive notification about *The One Minute Millionaire* book.

10. The authors will be available for a major media tour to promote the book.

The media track record of MVH and RGA is impressive. They have been on virtually every major talk show and thousands of minor ones—some several times.

We propose the hiring of a major outside firm such as Arielle Ford (who handles Deepak Chopra) to handle the PR for this book. One idea would be to pick the top local talk shows in our top 20 markets and agree to do Money Makeovers—a series of dramatic before/after demonstrations of the effects of implementing *The One Minute Millionaire* in the lives of individuals.

Most Americans—including talk show hosts—are hopelessly muddled and confused when it comes to handling their money. They will welcome information that clears up the muddle and shows them how they can quickly achieve financial peace of mind.

MVH and RGA can split up to do twice as many PR appearances in the same time. Here's a typical opening tease for a local talk show with RGA:

> In the eighties and nineties, he showed America how to make big money in real estate, and there are thousands of millionaires nationwide to prove it. Now he's back with a revolutionary new program he calls the One Minute Millionaire. Our guest is Robert Allen, and when Robert Allen talks, it's not just talk. He

> delivers. Today three lucky members of our studio audience will be selected to have a Money Makeover with Robert Allen personally to prove that anyone can gain control of their finances in 24 hours or less and be on their way to financial security in 21 days—maybe even a millionaire in less than a year. Please welcome Mr. Robert Allen.

What's nice about the Money Makeover idea is that it automatically builds in a second appearance on the same show—perfect for building momentum.

In addition to media events, both MVH and RGA will conduct seminars in each targeted city. These live seminars, coupled with live local media, can be very effective in driving book sales in local markets. RGA recently completed a 22-city PR tour for *Multiple Streams of Income.* In each city, he spoke to 2 audiences per day at free seminars. The seminars were filled by a targeted direct mail campaign to 600,000 people, which announced the release of the book and offered a free seminar. At each of these free seminars, a local bookstore was invited to sell books to audience members. In six of the top book markets, RGA spoke at the Learning Annex.

Did this overall strategy work? *Multiple Streams of Income* launched on April 6 and hit the *New York Times* business best-seller list five weeks later. It has sold almost 100,000 copies and rising.

A similar strategy will be employed in the launching of *The One Minute Millionaire.*

11. We will be launching the OMM Investment Game. Cardinal Industries developed and published a Chicken Soup for the Soul game. It became the fourteenth best-selling game of 1999. With the help of Cardinal Industries once again, we plan on developing a money-themed game based on the *OMM* book. Robert Kiyosaki, of *Rich Dad Poor Dad*, has also used this approach with great success.

We are also considering an investment challenge similar to the popular *USA Today* investment game The Investment Challenge. Readers are invited to select an imaginary $100,000 portfolio of stocks and mutual funds. The best-performing portfolio in six months wins the top prize, such as a vacation for two in Europe.

This is a natural idea for *The One Minute Millionaire.* Readers will have the opportunity to win prizes by using *One Minute Millionaire* strategies.

12. We will get dozens of influential, high-profile people to endorse OMM.

13. We will arrange for selected sponsors to donate valuable prizes to be awarded to readers.

In addition to valuable prizes, some lucky reader could even win $1 million (over twenty years) just for reading *OMM* and answering a few simple questions. The final prize will be determined by the number of sales, with a maximum prize of $1 million awarded to one incredibly lucky reader. All of this, of course, must be orchestrated carefully to create excitement without losing respectability and legitimacy—in the same way that *Reader's Digest* does it.

14. We will arrange for sponsors to give valuable coupons for discounts worth up to $10,000 for various products and services.

We want the decision to buy OMM to be a no-brainer. Readers will be offered a secret pass code offering access to valuable discount offers on the OMM website.

We see $10,000 worth of money-saving coupons honored by dozens of national companies like Hertz, Procter & Gamble, Century 21, Sears, Fidelity Investments, and Merrill Lynch.

There could even be a One Minute Millionaire card giving the bearer instant discounts at participating retailers. Hollywood includes these kinds of tie-ins every time they make a movie. Why not do it with a book?

15. We will create valuable exposure for OMM by tie-ins with major charities.

A portion of the proceeds from the sale of OMM directly goes to promotional partners and charities. Because they directly benefit from the success of the book, they are motivated to promote it to their constituencies.

The goal is to raise $10 million for charity from the sale of OMM: $1 from each book goes to charity = $10 million.

16. We will run full-page ads in dozens of magazines.

We envision dozens of national magazines carrying full-page ads promoting "The One Minute Millionaire" seminar. Prominent in the ads will be the announcement about the book. We have already made arrangements with *Millionaire Magazine* for such a promotion. This results in thousands of sales of the OMM book.

17. We will drop millions of pieces of direct mail.

The OMM seminar will also be promoted though millions of pieces of targeted direct mail. Each piece will include an announcement about the book. This will result in thousands of additional sales.

18. We will announce the forthcoming book in all of our ongoing business activities, business cards, stationery, direct mailings, websites, speeches, brochures, audio programs, and newsletters.

19. We will create a groundswell of positive word of mouth for OMM.

Of all the marketing vehicles—television, radio, direct mail, newspaper, special promotions—nothing is ultimately as powerful as word of mouth. According to studies, a dissatisfied customer will complain to seventeen friends. A satisfied customer will only tell three friends, but those three friends are very important. How do you get book readers to tell those three friends?

It all starts with an excellent product. The book had better deliver on its promise. Advertising and promotion is the kick-start to get people talking—but if the book is bad, the game is over. Obviously *The One Minute Millionaire* had better be one great book. And it will be.

20. We will create incentives for readers to recommend or give the book as a gift.

If you want people to do something, you've got to tell them what to do and reward them for doing it. How do we get people to recommend *The One Minute Millionaire* to their friends? Here is a sample paragraph that might be included in the book's introduction:

> Walt Disney once said, "Do what you do so well that when people come to see what you do they'll want to come again and bring their friends." If you like the book, if it works for you, all we ask is that you tell a

friend. In fact, we've made it easy for you. In the back of the book is a coupon for 10 percent off the price of this book. We simply ask that you pass that coupon on to one of your friends. After all, friends don't let friends pay retail. And if you're thinking about a special gift for Christmas, graduation, or a birthday, what better way to say "I appreciate you" than to give your friends and family the gift of financial success?

21. We will establish affiliations with 100 local OMM partners in 100 cities.

This idea is potentially the most important concept of the entire marketing plan. In each of 100 major markets, we will establish relationships with 100 local merchants and service providers who will help us promote the *OMM* book. In each city, there are at least 100 businesses and individuals who will benefit from the sale of OMM. For example, local stockbrokers, investment advisors, realtors, Internet service providers, and web designers will pay for the privilege of being listed as an approved One Minute Millionaire service provider. The cost for this relationship is the agreement to buy 100 books *in advance* of the publication date. Then these merchants will agree to offer the book to their top clients and customers as a gift. During the PR tour, MVH and RGA will hold private seminars with these 100 local sponsors and a few of their top clients.

Therefore in each city, there will be prepaid orders for 10,000 books. Multiply this by 100 cities and you have 1 MILLION presold books.

Is this possible? We believe that we can do something that has never been done in publishing history: to deliver *prepaid* orders for 1 million books before the publication date. The word of mouth and advance publicity would create a groundswell of excitement and curiosity.

22. We will use bypass marketing to get this book into unusual places.

Chicken Soup for the Soul became a publishing phenomenon because the authors were willing to think outside the box. This meant offering the book at dozens of nontraditional book outlets. We have sold tens of thousands of books at truck stops, bakeries, grocery stores, clothing stores, minimarts, nail technicians, chiropractors, dentists, hospital gift shops, cruise ships, and restaurants. We call this *bypass marketing* because it bypasses the traditional bookstore model.

MVH and RGA will build on this pioneering effort and find dozens of nontraditional outlets for *The One Minute Millionaire* book. For example, we have already developed a relationship with distributors who sell Disney videos through drugstores and grocery stores.

23. We will pursue major corporate tie-ins.

Through years of speaking to large corporate clients, MVH and RGA have developed relationships that open doors for major corporate tie-ins for this book. For example, financial institutions will find that this book contains brilliant information that is perfectly suited for their investment clients. Insurance companies, mutual fund houses, banks, and major telecommunications companies have already approached us, asking us to create targeted educational content for their customers. We have no doubt that many of these contacts will bear excellent fruit.

24. We will take care of the gatekeepers so they will take care of us.

MVH has been very successful at targeting the gatekeepers who have the opportunity to influence the sale of Chicken Soup books to the ultimate customer. For example, he has been invited to speak to the staff of Ingram and bought breakfast for its entire staff of 126 phone sales personnel. Such humble gestures really do have an impact on sales! MVH has done the same at Books-A-Million with similar results. Both MVH and RGA will be available for targeted speeches for the staffs of all of the major gatekeeper companies such as Borders, Barnes and Noble, Books-A-Million, and Amazon.

25. We will send a weekly fax blast to all bookstores nationwide.

Chicken Soup was able to maintain awareness at nationwide bookstores by sending a weekly fax blast to every one of the thousands of bookstores across the country. The same strategy will be used with *The One Minute Millionaire.*

26. We will pursue licensing arrangements with vigor.

MVH understands licensing like perhaps no other author. *Chicken Soup* generates millions of dollars of revenue and massive amounts of exposure through dozens of individual licensing arrangements with companies nationwide. The licensed products include dolls, games, T-shirts, clothing, toys, calendars (a top selling item in 1999), and more.

Chicken Soup Enterprises employs a team of savvy licensing experts to extend licensing to dozens of new companies each year.

Licensing of the OMM brand will be a major focus. It will generate massive exposure with zero marketing expense.

27. We will target and have a presence on the major airlines.

We will pursue articles in major airline magazines and audio content in the airline's audio channel as well as in each airport's bookstores. Airline travelers are a prime target for this book.

28. We intend on bringing OMM to movie theaters worldwide.

Ordinarily publishers are wary of potential movie tie-ins because the odds of producing a feature-length film are extremely low. But what if the movie could be completely sold out before opening night? You'll have to read the marketing plan for the OMM movie to see how we plan on making Hollywood history.

At the very least, let's just say that if the movie ever does get made, it certainly won't hurt book sales!

A Final Comment

Obviously there are hundreds more ideas to help turn *The One Minute Millionaire* into the biggest money book in a generation. In the future, when people in the industry talk about the enormous success of this book, they will say that one of the key factors was that the coauthors were a marketing and promotional dream team.

We hope that you can sense how passionate we are about this book and its message of hope and financial freedom. We know it can positively influence the lives of millions. We are looking for a publisher who is equally passionate about the success of this book.

A book like this with a team of marketing-savvy authors doesn't come along very often. Are you ready to make history with us?

Amazing Benefits for Buyers of 100 Books

Robert Allen and I wanted to create some special benefits for people who bought 100 copies of *The One Minute Millionaire*. Here's what we came up with:

As an advance purchaser of 100 copies of *The One Minute Millionaire*, you get:

1. 100 books to give as gifts to clients and friends.
2. A 50 percent discount on all of the books.
3. 100 grateful clients and friends.
4. The possibility of earning reciprocal business because of your generosity. *You get what you give.*
5. A copy of the book personally autographed by MVH and RGA.
6. A personal welcome note from MVH and RGA.
7. A photo with MVH and RGA.
8. Three valuable special reports created by MVH and RGA.
9. A certificate of membership: "You Are One in a Million!"
10. A one-day seminar with MVH and/or RGA in your city (one of 100 cities) (a value of $995).

11. A three-day Millionaire Retreat with MVH and RGA in a resort destination (a value of $2,995).
12. A live "Cash in a Flash" teleconference with MVH and RGA.
13. A live "Cash in a Flash " online chat with MVH and RGA.
14. A listing on our web page as a VIP member of the "One" network.
15. A personal endorsement from MVH and/or RGA for your book, project, or product (depending upon certain conditions).
16. Secret access code to our "One and Only" Internet library.
17. A bundle of special favors from OneWorldLive .com.
18. Membership in Oceans Alive, a movement to preserve our oceans.
19. A listing of your name in *The One* book.
20. A list of our 100 top recommended websites.
21. A ticket to *The One* play (assuming it happens).
22. Our list of the 21 most influential books.
23. Our list of the 10 most powerful tapes.
24. Our list of the 100 most important contacts: the Power Rolodex.
25. Our list of the 100 must-see locations in the world.
26. A list of valuable free items from our sponsors.

27. Our CD-ROM, jam-packed with valuable information, digital books, coupons, and more.
28. A complete marketing plan for *The One* book.
29. One free classified ad for your product, service, or idea on The One website.
30. A One membership card, entitling you to valuable discounts and special offers.
31. A One credit card from an e-bank.
32. A free financial fitness checkup.
33. A free health screening.
34. One free emotional screening.
35. One free share in The One IPO.
36. An invitation to accompany us on our world tour when we launch The One internationally.
37. An invitation to participate in the PR tour for *The One*.
38. The tools to set 101 goals.
39. A chance to win/earn the $1 million prize.
40. The chance to win one of $10 million life insurance policies.
41. The chance to be an extra in *The One* movie.
42. The chance to spend a day with MVH and/or RGA. "A Day in the Life of . . ."
43. The chance to earn $1,000 by submitting the best marketing idea to sell 1 million books.
44. The chance to be one of 100 people who win membership in the 3 percent club ($7,500 value).

45. The chance to be one of 100 people who participate in RGA's Protégé Program ($4,995 value).
46. The chance to win a trip to Italy and 1 million lire.
47. The chance to be one of 100 who win free tuition to MVH Speak and Write Conference ($500 value).
48. The chance to be selected for a Marketing BrainTrust consultation by MVH and RGA.
49. The special report on the Marketing BrainTrust consultation.
50. The opportunity to help build a house for Habitat for Humanity.
51. The opportunity to help out "below-zero" kids.
52. The opportunity to participate with MVH and RGA at *USA Today*'s Make a Difference Day.
53. The opportunity to participate with MVH and RGA in donating 1 million pints of blood.
54. The opportunity to become a trainer for The One seminar.
55. The opportunity to meet Wyland, the world's greatest marine artist, at one of his book signings.
56. The opportunity to meet the 100 most influential people on the planet.
57. The opportunity to donate 1 million pennies to the charity of your choice.
58. The opportunity to participate in history: the largest and most hyped book presale in history.
59. The opportunity to meet the publisher of *The One*.

60. The opportunity to be the person(s) we make famous.
61. The opportunity to interview RGA and MVH one-on-one.
62. The opportunity to have MVH or RGA speak at your group for free.
63. The opportunity to write an endorsement for *The One.*
64. The opportunity to list your business in the back of *The One.*
65. The opportunity to be a paid speaker at an event held by MVH or RGA.
66. The right of first refusal to buy 100 tickets for the movie *The One.*
67. The right to be the first to test The One game.
68. The right to participate and get the results of The One survey.
69. The right to receive special discounts on all MVH and RGA information products for life.
70. The right to be the first to read the manuscript for *The One* and offer feedback.
71. The right to market *The One* products and programs internationally.
72. The right to participate in *The One* community chat room.
73. The right to generate publicity in your home city as a member of The One club.

74. The right to be at the launch of *The One* book when we release 10,000 butterflies.
75. A group photo of those who attend the butterfly release.
76. First notification for all MVH and RGA projects, products, and programs.
77. An invitation to the Horatio Alger banquet to rub shoulders with world's top entrepreneurs (banquet and fees not included).
78. The realization that you are helping to eradicate financial illiteracy.
79. The realization that you are helping men and women in rescue missions nationwide.
80. The realization that you are part of an exclusive group.

One Final Bonus Idea

I have been teaching how to effectively market books for twenty years at my seminars. I have had the best of the best authors, speakers, teachers, and thinkers present how they did it as writers and marketers. I humbly invite you to attend my MEGA BOOK MARKETING SEMINAR for $997 on my website and promise you: if you watch these videos, one per week for a year, they will inspire you to profound results in writing, in your career or profession, and in your personal life. Drinking in the wisdom of the masters is always a magnificent idea. The richest man in America is Warren Buffett. At his Berkshire Hathaway investors' meeting, I heard him say, "The best investment you can ever make is in yourself!"

PART FIVE

The Power of Social Networking: A Whole New Way to Sell

In marketing, social networking could become bigger than the Big Bang, because everyone can do it for FREE. *Free* is the new magic buzzword in marketing. It grabs readers' attention and draws people into checking out your offering. On sites like Twitter and Instagram, you can post virtually all nonpornographic content for free. This levels the playing field. Beginners with imagination, creativity, and originality have as much chance of hitting a grand slam business homerun as a Fortune 500 company. Ideas win in social networking. Anyone, including you, can have the next big idea.

We've been looking at some important information—how to get your book written and how to get it out into the world. But for excitement and potential profitability, NOTHING compares to what we're going to discuss here in part 5.

There has never been anything like this on the marketing radar—everything from websites like YouTube to social networking sites such as Facebook and Twitter. By the time you read this, countless new social networking sites will dominate cyberspace. Just think about it: once you learn how to navigate these sites (which is not difficult), you can build your own database of people who can exponentially expand awareness of you, your book, and whatever else you create.

Networking on that level used to require a lot of time, skill, and money; now it's free!

In fact, "send no money" is one of the defining elements of social networking sites.

They *have* to be free, or they're not truly social networking websites. The business model of the sites themselves is built on maximizing traffic, which is the number of first-time and repeat users. If users have to pay to get on the website, their numbers will be severely limited. In other words, there probably won't be any. (Most of these free websites make money from advertising, not membership fees. This excludes information-based websites, like ESPN, which charge a nominal fee for special insider privileges, such as stats and reports, that are not available to general users.)

Social networks are attractive to businesses because consumers are connecting with other consumers, so trust tends to be higher. Secondly, there's a tremendous amount of media buzz about this newest form of marketing. Lastly, there are lots of folks using social networks. In 2007, according to Forrester Research, about two-thirds of all American youth used at least one social networking website daily, and about one-third of U.S. adults used one as least once a month. The figures are sure to be higher now.

Staying up to speed is a daily challenge for all of us in the information age. Incorporating new communication habits is a stretch. But when you realize that, instead of purchasing ad space or hiring a PR firm, you can market yourself for free from your living room in the amount of time it takes to write a tweet.

There's a lot to be grateful for with regard to technology. So say thanks, and get to work.

Once upon a time, artists needed to partner with managers and agents in order to get their work seen. Once upon that same time, authors needed agents, publishing houses, and bookstores in order to get their work known. Not anymore. You have the power now, at the click of a keypad, to be not only an author, but also a PR company, a publisher, an agent, and a speaker.

The biggest mistake you can make is to say that you just want to be the writer and let everyone else do all that other stuff. If you do that, you will be sharing your pie with a bunch of people who all want large slices and who will leave you with very little in the end.

Be a geek. Be a proud geek. Or find a geek with whom to partner up. Get on the computer and maximize your social networking efforts so that everyone can see your brilliance and the importance of your message. If you are a senior citizen, have your kids, grandkids, or public library teach you the basics. See them as resources that are tuned in, plugged in, and turned on to this phenomenon. If you taught your kids to read, it's time to let them teach you to prosper in the new economy that can potentially include everyone.

I say it could *potentially* include everyone, because I believe the mobile iPhone and its equivalents are the device of convergence. This new generation of phones instantly sends and receives text, audio, and video. Thanks to this amazing technology, you have 7 billion potential customers. One million ways to make a million bucks will be next in the evolution of this technology. Toward this end, thousands of applications for the iPhone and its cousins are coming into being. One such application was created by Joel Comm, my friend, colleague, and teacher at our Mega Marketing Seminars. Joel conceived and delivered an application called i-fart. It went viral immediately. It was the silly eighth-grade humor that took hold. It cost 99 cents, and millions wanted to download the application immediately to use on their unsuspecting friends and relatives. I witnessed this firsthand within days of its release, and several of us at lunch had a big and memorable laugh.

Another powerful social marketing activity is purchasing domain names. The king of domain names is Marc Ostrofsky, my great friend and writing partner. Marc has created and/or purchased 362,000 domain names. He sold the name *biz.com* for $7.2 million with a rider in his contract that said if it resold, he would get an additional 10 percent—which he did receive when biz.com resold for $345 million. Marc's company grosses $50 million annually with blinds.com, and $5 million with cufflinks.com. As I write this, Marc and I are finishing a new book tentatively titled *How to Make Money Starting with No Money.* (Remember: make lists of killer titles!)

There's absolutely no limit to what you can accomplish in our new interconnected world. You'll be able to sell anyone, anywhere, anytime on your mobjet.com account. You'll know in hours—even minutes—whether you are addressing the buying needs of your target market. For writers and book marketers, this is truly the Golden Age of new possibilities.

Social Networking Has Changed the Game Forever!

The power of the Internet has fundamentally transformed the way people interact with each other—in everything from finding a spouse to booking an airline ticket. If you're not up to speed with the web technologies we're going to be discussing, you're missing the best opportunities that have ever existed for getting your book out into the world. Sign up for them! You have a chance to reach a massive number of people in an incredibly short period of time. So get on board with social networking in a big way. It's not just worth your time; it's absolutely essential to your success.

The best way to go about it is to not overwhelm yourself. In the following sections, I am going to discuss several different social networking websites. The worst thing you could do is sign up for all of them at once. Far better strategy: sign up for one, get to know it, and then when you feel fluent with it, sign up for another social networking opportunity. That way, you will also get to know your own personal preferences as well. You might discover you are a Facebook person and not a Twitter person or vice versa. The most important thing is to make these sites work for you and not the other way around.

Be Clear about What Really Matters

Nothing like social networking has existed in the past. Still, at least some classic truths apply. For example: pure talent is not enough! Many talented writers—or talented athletes, or talented musicians—believe that their God-given abilities will bring success on their own. But the truth is this: talent only determines the upper limit of how far you can go. Whether you actually reach that upper limit depends on lots of other factors.

The good news is that most, if not all, of the determining factors mentioned above are within your control. When you're marketing yourself on the Internet, displaying your talent is not enough. You can't simply post selections from your book, no matter how brilliant those selections may be. You've got to use the tools of electronic media in a careful, cunning way. There's an infinite amount of content on social networking sites! Getting the attention you deserve takes patience and persistence. There's a lot more to it than just saying, "Look at me!"

Monetizing Social Networks

Just for fun, try thinking of your business as a solar system. You are the sun, and your work is the sunlight. Close to you are your inner planets; Mercury, Venus, and Earth, which represent loyal customers who will be with you all your life and will sign up for everything you do.

Then there are your midrange planets, Saturn and Jupiter, representing customers who have bought something from you at one time and probably will buy something from you again in the future.

Last are your outer planets, Uranus and Neptune. They are still within your gravitational pull. They have never bought anything from you before. They might never buy anything from you. But should they still feel your light? Absolutely! In other words, you should be generously and continually offering your gifts to them so that eventually these outliers will feel compelled to migrate closer to your inner circle.

The mistake people make with social networking websites is believing that the moment they join, fifty outliers will immediately become inner planets. Unfortunately, such thinking is common on the web. You will frequently come into contact with—and be annoyed by—sales pitches from individuals chatting endlessly about their books and products.

Whether you are selling a book or doing events, the best way to make money from social networking sites is to get people to sign up for your database. In earlier sections, I discussed one way to do that: offer a free sample chapter of your book in order to entice visitors to give you their name and email address. The freebie you offer can be anything—get creative! Many of your colleagues will cheerfully give you enticing electronic gifts for you to distribute to your clients and customers, because it expands their own bases.

As you get busy with social networking, I recommend an outer-planet strategy. That means giving away tons of free useful information on your topic. Just keep giving. In fact, you might give away 80 percent of your information up front. I know that sounds high, but here's how people think: "Wow, if this is the free information, the information I have to pay for must be incredible." They see you're the real deal. They get hooked on your free advice and get excited to participate in what you are doing.

This is monetizing the social network. On one hand, we're dealing with a new technology, but on the other hand, many of the things that have always been true of business are still true here, such as the importance of building relationships with your customers.

Coming onto a social networking site with guns blaring, pasting your Amazon URL into every post so that people will buy your book, is a strategy for burning out your friends.

Just a note: if you can get word of mouth (a buzz) going about you and your book and message, you won't have to depend solely on the customer who has just purchased from you. You want to keep building and expanding your relationships. Keep inviting your outer planets to migrate inward. Make people happy they know you.

Remember, it takes time to build a following, but if you have a great message, it is inevitable. Are you challenging your readers to open their minds and hearts? Are you inspiring them? Don't allow yourself to grow stagnant. Be creative. Be infinitely creative. The world needs your creativity.

There is nothing worse for a user than signing into a blog they are following only to discover that their favorite blogger has been offline for a week. They may try again in a day or two to see if anything new has been written. But you can pretty much guarantee that if they come back a third time and there is still nothing new, they're not coming back again. There are always a few loyal individuals who will stay with an RSS feed for an extended period of time regardless of posts, but most people are looking for new ideas and new inspiration. It's the reason they come to you, so be prepared to serve them. You might make a monthly list of new topics so that you don't get stale. Then stay active! No stagnant inventory! You need to stay recent on your posts and get people interacting with you. You want those interactions. Start thinking, "What's their takeaway? What am I giving people? How am I blessing them?"

Where's the Money?

The Internet has been called the second gold rush for a reason. But do not be deceived that it is easy, or else everyone doing it would be rich. That was true for a few short years in Silicon Valley, but not anymore.

There are four places where money comes and goes on the Web: purchases, advertising, sponsorship, and memberships.

Purchases could be anything from an antique clock on eBay to a book on Amazon to plane tickets to the Bahamas to a weekend workshop with your favorite author. Advertising is frequent around the Web, especially on sites that have strong traffic for click-through rates—that is, large numbers of people who click on the ad. But unless you have millions of users, it is challenging to bring in income through advertisers.

Sponsorship is relatively rare, but it can bring great money. For example, if a channel on YouTube is getting millions of views, Sony Pictures might be alerted and invite the creators to make a webisode, a minimovie to be shown on the Web, for their associated Internet site, Crackle, thereby sponsoring the artists who were previously posting for free. Or perhaps a one-legged runner starts a blog that suddenly captures the attention of millions of readers. He might find that Nike wants to sponsor him.

Paid memberships to Internet sites are relatively rare, because site viewers lose momentum when asked to input their billing information. ESPN has the best model, whereby the "insiders" pay for sports statistics and features they can't get any other way. The cost very small: about $4 per month. That may not sound like much, but if you can generate several million subscribers, this starts looking like a lot of money.

Membership has only a limited application to social networking: by definition, social networking is free. You might see some paid advertisements here and there, but they do not dominate the sites at all. Remember that. Be delicate with your posts. Respect the fact that people are there to socialize, have fun, and make new friends.

Learn by Doing

The people who created Facebook and Twitter worked hard to make them as simple as possible. Did they succeed? Well, the social networking sites *are* pretty simple, but they're not completely simple, which actually is part of their attraction. We'll talk about how to navigate these sites as efficiently as possible. But the best way to learn social networking is to just jump in and start using the sites. Explore the different options and find out how they work. See what you like and what you don't like. Look at other people's profiles and see which one's stand out in your mind. Keep an eye out for funny little icons at the bottom of pages and see where they lead. And don't feel you have to start marketing your book until you're thoroughly ready to use the sites to their full potential. That can't be done in an hour or two, but it definitely shouldn't take more than a few days—which is an incredibly short time considering all that social networking has to offer.

Social Network Marketing Really Is Social

In selling themselves to the Internet world, both MySpace and Facebook made *friend* an important word. Facebook users invite each other to be friends. In order to succeed as a social network marketer, you need to remember that social networking was not created to help writers sell their books. In fact, if you go about self-marketing in the wrong way, you can actually get kicked off the sites.

What works and does not work will keep changing fast. We are in the most accelerated times in human history. What works today is to send out twenty worthwhile and important messages and then following up with an invitation to your website, webinar, seminar, or book launch.

So approach social network marketing the same way you'd approach a group of interesting people you'd really like to know. You can't just walk in and start handing out copies of your book. You must engage in the normal give-

and-take of conversation before anyone will buy into you as an author. Your first task is to be an interesting person; on the Internet, that means knowing the rule of the medium and using them.

Maximize Your Marketing Advantages

Before the Internet, mass marketing was dominated by big companies and powerful organizations. It took a lot of money to buy advertising time on time on the major TV networks—much more money than was available to individual entrepreneurs. The networks carefully monitor how many people watch their programming, and the costs of marketing are priced on that basis. The more people watching, the higher the cost to the marketer.

It's a different ball game on the Internet, especially on the social networking sites. Nothing is less effective on Facebook than the conventional marketing that has dominated other media. Here, for the first time in history, the little guy has the advantage! The trick is to maintain that little guy identity at the same time as you're working to realize your biggest dreams

When Push Comes to Suck

In earlier forms of marketing, the hard sell could sometimes be effective. A marketer who wouldn't take no for an answer could sell a lot of products. The client would buy something just to get out of the store.

But on the Internet, getting out of the store couldn't be easier. A click of the mouse takes you to an entirely different universe, and another click blocks the hard-sell marketer forever.

That's why successful marketing on social networking sites requires sucking people toward you rather than pushing them in the direction of your product. You want to create a gravitational pull. You've got to make yourself interesting so that potential readers want to learn more. The forward movement has to come from them. Your task is just to create the positive energy—and to remember that the slightest hint of hard sell will bring about that dreaded click of the mouse.

Turn Weaknesses into Strengths

Social networking is great for reaching the maximum number of people in the shortest possible time, but it's terrible for conventional sales. It's good for creating awareness of who you are and what you've done, but it's a lot less effective for actually exchanging your product for money. This can work to your advantage if you understand that you're creating relationships, not just buyers. When you actually do build friendships, as Facebook suggests, your social networking friends will hopefully do your selling for you. You can inspire electronic word-of-mouth advertising that will be much more effective than any selling you could do on your own.

Give Maximum Attention to Key Sites

Nothing is more amazing about the Internet than how fast things change. In less than a year, YouTube went from nothing to hundreds of millions of users. MySpace opened up the whole new universe of social networking, though today it has fallen far behind Facebook (with over 2.45 billion users) and YouTube (with 1 billion views per day).

The Internet is constantly changing; by the time you read this, it will undoubtedly have changed again. But for the foreseeable future, the key social networking sites are Facebook, YouTube, LinkedIn, and Twitter. Those are the sites we'll be looking at in detail. Even if others supplant them in the very near future, the principles you'll learn by studying them are likely to become even more important.

Facebook: 2.45 Billion Users!

Facebook's business model is based on building traffic. Plain and simple, it's about getting as many users as possible. It's a party, not a trade show. Toward that end, Facebook is designed to prevent people from turning it into a marketing extravaganza. Make no mistake: there are many people who want to turn Facebook into exactly that. Here's one example: powerful robotic tools create massive lists of Facebook friends who can then be spammed to the max.

In your eagerness to reach as many people as possible on Facebook, be aware that you are being monitored by the site's antispamming police. You may just be looking for ways to build awareness of your book, but if you friend a hundred people in one day (or one hour), you're going to look like exactly what Facebook wants to avoid. So be patient. You'll see that Facebook has the technical potential to reach thousands of people almost instantly. But that doesn't mean you need to activate that potential, or even that you should. (And just so you know, Facebook caps off your friend limit at 5,000.)

Friendship First

Never forget that business model of social networking sites depends on their not being taken over by hustlers pitching their products and services. If you become too aggressive—in fact, if you become aggressive at all—you will get blocked, unfriended, and perhaps banned by the sites themselves. So be in touch with social networking friends on the basis of shared interests for a reasonable period of time before you get around to bringing your business into the picture. I can't overemphasize how important this is! People aren't on Facebook to be sold something. This doesn't mean they won't want to buy, provided you give enough time and information for that desire to naturally emerge.

How will it emerge? Imagine for a moment that you are having dinner in a lovely restaurant overlooking a bay. You are seated with a few friends near the bar, and tables fan out toward the water from where you are seated. Suddenly six people get up, run over to the windows, and start pointing and shouting, staring out over the water.

Will you be curious to see what is in the water? Will you maybe even leave your table to go and have a look?

If enough people get excited about something, you will naturally want to know about it. That is how human beings are designed. If someone laughs, we want to know what was funny. If your message is brilliant, and your book speaks your message well, people are going to get excited about who you are and what you are doing. It may look like a sales process, but it is actually inspiration and enthusiasm converging in your bank account.

Make Friends—and Add a Personal Message

Facebook provides an easy, permission-based system for inviting people to connect with your profile page—in other words, for becoming a Facebook friend. The first thing it does (and most social networking sites do this), is ask you for access to your email address book so you can connect with friends you already have. It makes it very simple to find all your friends and get started.

When you invite someone new to become a friend, you're given the option of including a personal message along with the invitation. You should always take advantage of this option. That doesn't mean you have to write an emotional letter about how much this connection means to you. In fact, you shouldn't write anything of the sort. Just a few sentences about why you'd like to connect with this person will make you stand out from the crowd. (Please do not include the link to buy your book on Amazon here.)

Very often you'll have found out about this person through a prior connection with a Facebook friend that you have in common (Facebook always displays that information), so mentioning your common friend is a good way to start the relationship. This will show that your connection was more than just the random pushing of a button. There are plenty of robotic programs doing just that, and you'll want to show you're not one of them.

Google Every Name

Besides having friends in common, a little research on a potential friend can also go a long way. This is especially important with people you really want as a connection. First click on the picture of the person who is asking to be your friend, which will take you to their profile page, where you can learn about them. Then Google the name, and follow up on whatever information you find. It's amazing how often you'll discover many meeting points. Schools attended, companies worked for, cities lived in, sports teams followed—all of these can be the basis for something more than a hit-or-miss friend request.

Statistical evidence has validated the principle of six degrees of separation. Whether it's an Inuit fisherman living in the Arctic Circle or an aboriginal Australian in the outback, you are only six people away from a personal meeting with that individual. Use Internet search engines to explore those connecting points. Then use what you learn to widen your circle of friends and deepen it at the same time.

Make Your Profile Look Exciting

Once someone accepts you as a Facebook friend, they gain the ability to see your profile, which includes all the text, photos, videos, and personal interests that you choose to mention. You can also configure your profile so that it's open to everyone on Facebook even without a friendship connection (I definitely suggest you choose that option). After all, you have nothing to hide. On the contrary, you want the world to find out about you, and the sooner the better.

Creating your Facebook profile can be a fun and interesting task. Accept the constraints of its template—

you don't really have a choice. And even within those constraints, there's plenty of space for creativity.

A Picture Is Worth 1,000 Words

I don't need to tell you that the personal photo on your Facebook profile page is the most important part of the whole page, right? Use an image that's flattering, informal, and inviting. Too slick is even worse than too sloppy—and you should have more than one such image available! Underneath your profile picture there's a button where visitors can click to see more images. All of these should be good, so that you can easily rotate them from the archive to your main profile page. Make this rotation every week or two. You want your friends to see that your page and your Facebook personality are dynamic works in progress.

More important than mere pictures are videos. Peter Guber, with fifty Academy Awards for movies like *Rocky*, *Batman*, *Rain Man* and owner of the Golden State Warriors and Los Angeles Dodgers, told me that everything is going to become videocentric telephonically. So be a conscious video creator. Look at my Facebook, LinkedIn, and other sites for ideas.

Also, please note that with the advance of 5G we will soon have three-dimensional avatars being emitted out of our phones by the end of 2020, according to Verizon CEO Hans Vestberg. You will be in one place, broadcasting what looks like you to multiple phones. It will be like a Zoom call on steroids.

The other master of this soon-to-be reality is the chairman of Singularity University, Dr. Peter Diamandis, author of *The Future Is Faster Than You Think*. See him online and watch his YouTube presentations, and you'll become convinced that the future is near. You'll also be amazed at the technology that will quickly improve our lives and lifestyles.

Make sure that your profile page offers visitors lots of pictures to see—but not too many. Facebook displays the number of images in each folder. If, as sometimes happens, that number is in the high hundreds, you're sending a message of self-absorption, which is not what you want. Be selective. If your digital camera is your constant companion, as we suggested earlier, you should have plenty to choose from. Include pictures not only of yourself, but of you with other people your friends might be interested in. Celebrities are good, but don't overdo it. Animals are good too—and if you can find a celebrity animal, you can really hit a home run!

Branding Yourself without Branding Yourself

By now, it's probably clear that the key to social network marketing is to make it as unlike conventional marketing as possible. Yes, your purpose in being on the network is getting your book to the largest possible number of people. But that purpose is best served when you're conversational, informal, and energetic—without being overwhelming. There are dozens of opportunities for this on your Facebook profile. Explore the profiles of people who interest you and you'll learn a lot about how this works.

Again, be aware of how important your pictures really are—not only the pictures themselves, but also the text you create to accompany them. When you upload a picture, Facebook provides a box in which you can type a caption. People who visit your page are *always* going to look at your photos, and consequently they're *always* going to read the captions. Take this opportunity to share bits and pieces of information about yourself that will add up to a positive and interesting mosaic of you and your work. An individual caption shouldn't read like a résumé, but all of them together should make up something very much like one.

In addition to your image library, the Facebook profile has a space for sharing your interests and hobbies. You should definitely feature your book in this space. Be sure to mention the title! Embed this information with references to other interests and hobbies your readers are likely to share. For example, if you've written a book about rock climbing, there's a good chance your readers will also connect with wilderness preservation and outdoor life in general. Make it clear that you share those interests as well. You should come across as someone your Facebook friends want to hang out with. That's got to happen before they'll want to buy from you.

As with your main picture, keep updating your profile information. Don't let anything get stale. Your profile page indicates the last date your information was updated. Don't let that date be more than a month old; better yet, don't let it be more than a couple of weeks.

Make Yourself Visible

As you learn more about how Facebook profile pages are set up, you'll see that the privacy settings offer several options. If you just wanted to connect with close personal friends, you might want to be discreet. But that's not why you're here, so make your information as visible as possible across the site.

Moreover, there should be *plenty* of such information. The longer people spend reading about you, the more progress you're making toward creating a relationship that translates into readership and sales. If there's little or no personal information in your profile, people will have no choice but to conclude you don't have much to say. That's not exactly the way a writer wants to be seen. From the point of view of the site itself, a lack of information will red-flag you as a potential spammer who has created a network of shell accounts. In that case, your profile may get deleted as well as ignored.

The More the Merrier?

As you get used to looking at different Facebook profiles, become aware of the elements that always catch your attention. The photographs will definitely be at the top of the list. Beyond the pictures, most people also look at the friends list and the number of friends that the profile's owner has been able to amass. The more friends you have, the cooler (or hotter) you must be, right?

On that assumption, many Facebook users try to make their friends list as extensive as possible. There are plenty of lists with thousands of names. But growing your friends list just for the sake of growing it is misplaced energy. It's much more important to keep in touch with the contacts you do have, regardless of how high that number may be. How responsive are you to your friends? How responsive are they to you? The answer to those questions will be "not very" if your list is more than a few hundred names. But if you're connecting with those few hundred people in an enthusiastic, informative, and pro-active way about yourself and your book, they'll do the rest of the work for you. Your friends will talk about you with their friends, and that elusive goal of viral marketing will be yours. If you haven't exchanged a message with someone on your friends list for several months, try getting in touch to see what happens. If nothing happens, it might be time to unfriend that person from your bloated list. And the time has definitely arrived when you see names without having any memory of who those people actually are.

Your First Three Hundred Friends Are the Most Important

There are a couple of bars in the upper left-hand menu of Facebook. One says "Home," one says "Profile," one says "Friends," and the last says "Inbox." Under the Home section, you have a chance to see the news feed of all your friends. You will learn what they are up to, what they are interested in, what videos and songs they like, and they might even ask for your opinion or ideas from time to time on their projects and thoughts. If you make friends with people you are already friends with in life, this will keep you closer to them on a daily basis. If you befriend strangers, you will have a chance to get to know people with whom you would not ordinarily come into this kind of intimate contact.

Your first three hundred friends are the most important, because these are the folks you are going to stay connected to the most. Pay attention to what they are up to.

Check in every day. Learn about them. And participate in what they have to say. The more value you add with your presence, the more people will appreciate you and have positive feelings about you and what you bring them.

Restrict How Many Friends You Add per Day

Sometimes writers are so excited about social network marketing that they can't believe their eyes. Just think of it: instead of being holed up in a garret scribbling away, a writer can now access hundreds of people with just a few keystrokes. It seems as if there's no limit to the number of friend invitations you can send out in a day, in an hour, or even in a minute.

But there actually is a limit. Not that anyone knows exactly what it is, because the number is a Facebook secret. But you should not send out more than fifty invitations per day, or you'll look like a robot. Or maybe you'll just look like an overzealous first-time author. Either way, Facebook may warn you about violating the site's terms of service. Repeated violations can result in the deletion of your account.

A Good Way to Get Attention

It's a principle of network marketing that certain people are "connectors." They're points of high energy from which hundreds or even thousands of other people draw inspiration and information. By putting yourself in touch with those people, you can make yourself visible to everyone who shares your interest.

This won't happen by itself. Bob Dylan and Sheryl Crow do have Facebook pages—but who's really behind those pages is another question. Connecting with the connectors can take some research and persistence. Still, if your message gets a response from Bob Dylan, thousands of people are going to see it if you've configured your privacy setting to "open."

Bob Dylan is an extreme example. While it's unlikely (though not impossible) that Bob is tapping away at his keyboard, someone less famous but more congruent with your interests might be much more available. Who are the real connectors in your subject area? What can you share that will grab their interest and elicit a response? Get that information and act on it!

Fan Pages versus Profiles

A popular application on Facebook you can use to your advantage is called "pages," also known as "fan pages." When you first sign up to Facebook, you will automatically create a profile. But now you can also create a page. A fan page lets people know more about who you are in your more public persona. The most notable difference between these two types of exposure on Facebook is that on your profile, you can only add 5,000 friends; on your page, an infinite number of people can become your fans, and you can update them about whatever you are up to. Many authors use fan pages to tell readers about their book releases and book tours. You can also post fun tidbits: quizzes related to your subject, or bonus chapters to your books to entice people.

Definitely create both a profile and fan page; experiment with how you want to divide your friends between the two. For example, you might want to use your profile only to connect with people you have met in person and use your fan page for all strangers. Or you might want to use your profile to connect with both your friends and the friends of your friends, building your network. How you go about screening people is up to you.

When you create a fan page for yourself, be sure to post to it often so that it shows activity. If people want to become your fan but click on your fan page and see that you haven't updated it since the Stone Age, they'll probably reconsider.

On Facebook, you can create a fan page by navigating to the lower left-hand menu and clicking on the tiny (and I mean really tiny) icon called "Ads and Pages."

Don't Join Too Many Groups

One of Facebook's most popular features is joining or creating groups of friends who have a shared interest. The site offers thousands of groups based on just about everything imaginable.

The groups you choose to join are important for several reasons. First, it's obvious that by joining a group that aligns with your interests, you'll come in contact with people who will want to read your book. So if you've written about the spiritual joys of fly-fishing, a group called "Spiritual Fly-fishers" will be a fitting choice! But there's more to it than that. Unless you disable the function, the groups you belong to will be displayed in your profile. Your selection of groups can make you more (or maybe less) interesting to potential friends.

Some people join hundreds of groups. If you go this route, you will look like exactly the kind of eager beaver most people on Facebook want to avoid—and you'll also attract the attention of the site's antirobotic monitoring systems. So find a reasonable number of groups that really interest you and join them for that reason. Make yourself an active participant in those groups, and the marketing of your book will start to happen by itself.

Launching a Group Is Easy

Once you have a large—but not too large!—network of Facebook friends, you can think about starting a group that's based specifically on your book. Before you do this, you should have made your friends aware of your book in just the right way: conversational, informal, and informative. In your messages to your friends, mention the possibility of starting a group before you actually do it. Mention it more than once. That way, when you actually start the group, you should have a number of people ready to join it immediately. No one wants to be the first diner in an empty restaurant. A group that has only one person in it (you) isn't likely to attract a lot of new members. So plant the seeds early.

Once your group is established, it can become your primary Facebook tool for developing interest and sales for your book. Here you can speak much more directly about your work than on the regular home page. Mention reviews, events, or signings connected with your publication. Don't try to sell the book directly on Facebook, but provide a link to your blog or website, where visitors will find a direct link to your book's page on Amazon. As with your profile page, update your book's group as often as you can. Show that a lot is happening with your project—because if you've done your marketing effectively, a lot *will* be happening every day.

One Message, Thousands of People

If you create your own group and get all your friends to join, you can message up to 5,000 people at once. This gives you a lot of power to develop an intimate relationship with a large number of people. As long as you share valuable content, people won't mind that you're promoting something. And in case they do mind, they can always leave your group and join another one. Remember that some websites that hold a database for you charge a monthly fee to keep in touch with this many people, and on Facebook it is totally free.

You may have heard me teach, "Get rich in a niche." The biggest and best niches have not even been thought of yet, and YOU can discover them! For example, Tom Sullivan—writer, actor, musician, and athlete—is blind. When he told me that his disability prevented him from getting health insurance, I decided to try to do something about that problem. And I have, through a company called 54 Million Freedom. We now offer insurance to millions of people around the world who have been denied health insurance because of handicaps. That's a lot of people! We even have an underground best seller called *54 Million Freedom* dedicated to this issue.

Giant untapped markets are waiting for YOU to discover them.

Perhaps because it's so easy to do, rapid growth on Facebook is a definite negative. It will have your account flagged immediately. This is not a race, so growing slowly and consistently is the way to go. Start now, even if your book is still in the inception phase. Gradually let people know who you are and how to connect with what you are doing.

You can even offer a monthly free event that you can tell people about on Facebook, whether it is a free webinar or in-person event. Just keep the ball rolling at a gradual pace so that people can start to experience your generosity as they get to know you and your message.

Another major rule that many people violate when making new friends is cutting and pasting messages. Adding a message to a friend request greatly increases the chance of getting accepted, but don't be tempted to use the exact same message for each new friend. Wherever you cut corners, it will come back to haunt (and hurt) you. Social networking is about intimacy. You want to create authentic relationships with people, and you cannot do that in a cookie-cutter way.

You Have to Be a Real Person

You can't advertise your business on a personal account, although I know a lot of people who are doing this. Under Facebook's terms of service, you are not allowed to directly advertise your business on a personal account. If you have placed your business logo on your profile picture, then you are definitely at risk of having your account disabled.

The Dangers of Messaging Too Many People

If you have a group or Facebook page with a large number of friends or fans, it's very easy to attract Facebook's antispam robots. These robots put a cap on how many messages you can send at one time and on how many people you can tag in a note. The robots want you to be socializing, not selling.

Beware of Phishing Scams

If you receive a message from Facebook asking for your password or any personal information, do not respond. This is a phishing scam—an attempt to capture your identity so that spam messages can be sent to all your friends and posted on their walls. Even though you did not initiate the spam, your account may be deleted until you offer an explanation.

Copyright Infringement Issues

Facebook will terminate the accounts of those who repeatedly publish copyrighted material on their profiles. That includes photos. If you find a photo on the web and you do not know the photographer, you need to contact the photographer of that picture and request the right to use it. Be diligent in your research.

Take Advantage of the Tagging Process

Tagging is a basic feature that Facebook provides for its users. If you post photos or notes, you are able to tag your friends. You can tag them for several reasons: to ask their opinion, to get their suggestions, to let them know you mentioned them in a note or that they appear in a photo, or to share what you are up to. Tagging makes people feel included, and it shows up on your home page and theirs, which will start to spread your message and identity. Have fun with it!

Host a Facebook Event

Email is already outdated in terms of sending out e-vites, or electronic invitations to events. Facebook has taken over, because it is so much quicker and more convenient. You can create an event, post a photo for it, and immediately invite everyone you know. Then you can keep track of who is coming, who is unsure, and who cannot make it.

As an author, you can start by giving a free book talk, or arrange a signing at a local bookstore when your book comes out. Remember, you're not just an author; think of yourself as a speaker too. When people see you on a stage holding your own book, an image is imprinted in their minds of who you are. So for the rest of their lives, they are going to think of your book whenever they think of you. You want that! Don't worry if you create an event and only your mother, your best friend, and your neighbor show up. Marketing statistics prove that people need to hear from you six times before they respond. So keep holding events, and I guarantee your efforts will gather speed and numbers.

The most important thing is to get out there and have fun with it. Your events don't need to be perfect. Just create an event and market it on Facebook, and get some practice speaking about your subject. You'll be surprised—you might enjoy it!

Explore Facebook Marketing

Facebook Marketing Solutions is a really brilliant (and free!) group on Facebook that teaches you how to market yourself and your work. The group uses examples in the major media, large and small, to give *you* ideas. They might show you a great idea that Pepsi Cola used recently, or take you to a website where a shoe company made a profit with a clever hook. Spend five minutes a day on this site, become a fan, and you will always have some new ideas on how to get yourself out there.

Twitter

Twitter is a free social networking and microblogging service that enables users to send and read updates (called "tweets"). Tweets are text-based posts of up to 140 characters in length, which are displayed on the user's profile page and delivered to other users who have subscribed to them (called "followers"). Senders can restrict delivery to those in their circle of friends or can, by default, allow anybody to access them. Users can send and receive tweets via the Twitter website, Short Message Service (SMS), or applications such as Tweetie, Twitterrific, Twitterfon, TweetDeck. The service is free to use over the Internet, but using SMS may incur phone service provider fees.

At this point, there are some 330 million active monthly users of Twitter. It is of unique value to marketers because it's more immediate and interactive than any other digital channel. It's easy to use Twitter's search to monitor conversations about your brand; marketers as diverse as Dunkin' Donuts, Comcast, and Dell use it to connect with fans, address support questions, and sell products. All marketers should look into Twitter; starting with securing your brand identity and monitoring existing chatter.

Twitter is different from Facebook in two ways. First, Twitter focuses more on businesses than on individuals, and, second, it allows you to connect with strangers more readily than Facebook does. That's a good thing. Twitter will help you cast your net broadly and over a long period of time. Lots of people are going to find out about you.

Use Twitter to Listen, Not Just Talk

This one is a maxim across the board in all social networking sites. Have you ever been cornered by a guy at a party with bad breath who introduces himself and then proceeds to tell you all about his business, his latest award, how his kids won the soccer tournament, and what trip he is about to take, all without learning your name?

Make Sure Your Profile Is Complete

Fill in all the fields (both required and optional), include the URL for your blog and/or website, and definitely upload a picture. Then start building your base of followers. Put the link "Follow me on Twitter" everywhere (your email signature, forums, website, and business cards.) Every time you post on your blog, invite people to follow you on Twitter.

Search for Twitter users whose follower base you would like to have for yourself. See who is following them and follow those users. They will follow you back. See who is following your friends and follow them. Twitter directories can help you find members who are likely to follow you. Examples include Just Tweet It and Twellow. Use Twitter's search feature to find profiles that interest you. Use Twitter's RSS feed to be notified every time a tweet containing a certain keyword goes out. Don't spam others about your book, or about anything. Follow other users. Be active in the community by posting comments about others' tweets. Only post useful and relevant information. Don't tweet every five minutes; once a day is plenty. Retweet (reply to others' tweets) often.

What Twitter Is and What It Isn't

Twitter is a social tool, not a classified advertising site. Craigslist is a extremely potent classified site that gets 50 million viewers every day.

Dean Graziosi, with whom I make infomercials, as I said above, discovered that he could make an extra

$1,000 or $2,000 every day buying locally and selling globally. He's putting into action the ideas that my friend Robby Smith revealed in his book called *Buy on Craigslist and Sell on eBay*. The book is available exclusively through Dean Graziosi's website. Robby Smith specializes in buying and selling in four areas he knows inside and out: bicycles, watches, toys, and auto parts and accessories. For instance, he bought a Pinarello bicycle for $375 on Craigslist and sold it hours later on eBay for $975—because he knew the value. He goes to garage sales and estate sales for fun and profit. Such opportunities can become income streams for everyone.

Balance Your Followers-to-Following Ratio

Try to maintain a balance between people you follow and people that follow you. If a lot of people follow you and you don't follow them, they will stop following you. If you are following plenty of people but just a few are following you, you'll be seen as a spammer trying to grow your follower base as quickly as possible.

Grow slow. Instead of adding two hundred new friends all of a sudden, add maybe fifty and wait for them to follow you back. Then follow another fifty. Use tools like Friend or Follow (friendorfollow.com). This is the best way to balance your ratio of followers to people you are following, and it takes just a few minutes.

Make It Worthwhile to Follow You

Tweet interesting stuff. Every time you are about to post something, ask yourself, "Is this something I would be fascinated by?" If the answer is no, chances are that your followers will feel the same way.

Here's an example of a piece of advice tweet:

You can get a red wine stain out of white carpet with one part Dawn liquid soap to one part hydrogen peroxide.

Here's an example of a fun social tweet:

Fell asleep immediately on the plane, woke up, and sneezed. Person next to me says, "Bless you." I looked over and it was a nun.

Here's a tweet to let people get to know you better:

I woke up this morning and watched the sunrise over the harbor with my old cat, Sammy, purring in my lap.

If you've written a book about how to plant a garden, this tweet might get your followers interested in your book:

If you want big, beautiful, fragrant roses, fertilize them with coffee grinds.

So you get the idea. It's best to mix it up. Be creative. Be personal, helpful, playful, and fun to know.

Learn from the Best

Find users with several thousand followers you'd would like to have, and learn from them. See what they are doing right and get ideas. Warren Buffett, an English major in college, is loved by everyone who reads his communications because they are brilliant, funny, and relevant, and share salient moneymaking insights that are instantly usable.

I also recommend looking at tweets from "zappos" (aka Tony Hsieh, CEO of Zappos Shoe Company). He manages to personalize his messages, let you know about his life, and keep you updated about his company in a playful, interesting, and engaging manner. OmniFocus software uses Twitter intelligently for tech and customer support. Their customers feel heard and cared about. What a gift!

First Give, Then Ask

What's true in all social networking is also true on Twitter. The majority of the people take, take, and take. They never give. Do things the other way around (the real spirit of social media), and you'll be noticed. Being stingy with your advice and ideas will not serve you. Be generous and others will appreciate you and show up for you.

Other Social Networking Sites

Are you overwhelmed yet? Well, take a deep breath. The most important element of the social networking process is finding what works for you. I encourage you to try everything on, and then stay with whatever seems like a fit.

LinkedIn

This is a professional website that is primarily for serious business connections. What makes it different from other social networking sites is that you are not allowed to connect with people you do not know. If you want to make a connection with someone, one of your connections must formally introduce you.

In this way, LinkedIn is similar to a networking party where you do not know anyone, and your friend takes you around and makes introductions for you. LinkedIn is great if you are looking for a job, looking to network with other professionals in your field, or seeking to establish a bit of status and reputation for yourself. People you know are allowed to recommend you, and you can accumulate recommendations from others who post on your page. LinkedIn is not a place to market your book per se, but it would be an excellent place to search for potential affiliates.

The primary content on your profile on LinkedIn will comprise your résumé and work experience. It is very important to be accurate and thorough, because this is how people are going to understand who you are. When you create your résumé, write it first in a Word document or a similar word-processing program and then copy and paste it into your LinkedIn profile.

YouTube

YouTube accounts for most of the traffic on the Internet. Did you catch that? YouTube accounts for most of the traffic on the Internet. That means if you are looking for visibility, this is your first stop.

It has never been easier or faster to create an account and start uploading videos to YouTube to get yourself seen and known online by millions of people. You can pick up very inexpensive video cameras, like the Flip camera, that are designed just for web video broadcasting, and in a matter of hours have your first video up and running.

Authenticity attracts people. Talking heads, not so much. But if your cat is weird, or you own a dancing pet bird, or you have just choreographed a wildly creative three-minute routine with a five-year-old and a monkey, you could be famous in a matter of hours.

YouTube can be challenging to monetize. The latest trend is for authors to create a book trailer, which is basically a movie trailer for your book. A book trailer gets people excited about what you have written by seeing it dramatically presented. You can also record yourself speaking in front of live audiences, which always helps to get you recognized as an expert.

The advertising world talks about brand advertising. In other words, the ads are not there to get you to buy something; they exist to make you aware of the brand. Think of YouTube that way. You want to make people aware of your existence. You are inviting them to get to know you.

As you invite people into your world, you might consider what makes you interesting. What will people identify with most in your message? How do you want to portray yourself?

For example, all your videos might be shot at the beach, or in your office, or holding your cat. Whatever makes *you* special should be in every video you make.

I am going to talk for a moment about some monumental YouTube videos that should be of interest to you. For example, one clip has been watched nearly 120 million times. It's called "History of Dance," and features one man who dances a timeline through history and, in a single routine, shows more dances than you can imagine.

Cats are very popular on YouTube. One video in particular is called "The Mean Kitty Song," and has been watched, as I write this, about 20 million times. It's a clever song that a musician wrote featuring, yes, you guessed it, his cat, filmed in his apartment, and well-edited so that it comes across as a low-end music video.

"Once Upon a Time in the Woods" is a video that Ben Arthur created with his younger brother, Julian. He then rotoscoped the video (which is a fancy way of saying he drew over the video frame by frame to create an artistic rendering) and had his dad add some folksy background music. YouTube loved his creativity and featured his video on its front page. Then a company in Japan saw it and hired Ben to work for them. He wasn't even out of college at the time!

Another big success is "Dear Leafs, I'm Breaking Up with You." In this clip a disgruntled fan creates a mock break-up scenario with a Canadian hockey team, the Toronto Maple Leafs. The video, filmed in his kitchen, quickly got more than 50,000 views. The video was featured in *USA Today*, and the creator became an immediate Internet celebrity.

Most people have never heard of Marina Orlova. But several hundred thousand people have subscribed to her ever-popular YouTube channel "Hot for Words." She is a linguist who uses a sexy approach to teaching her users about words, and she is very popular because of it.

Here's how it works. You shoot a video. You upload that video onto your computer. Once it is on your computer, you open one of the video editing programs for either the Mac or PC platforms. You can edit the video if you like, or you can keep it simple and just export it to the web. If you edit it, you can add titles, music, graphics, and anything else that inspires you. Videos should be under eight minutes long, and not bigger than ten megabytes.

Then log onto YouTube, create an account for yourself, and upload the video. Make sure your computer is connected to a power source, because uploading it can take a while.

You can also customize your channel, adding personal information and including your website and blog URLs. You want it to feel inviting to the kind of people who will be your customers.

Once your video is up, send an email to your list, or post it in your newsletter. You can also add a YouTube video share link to your Facebook page and include it there too.

Once your video is up on YouTube, how can you get people to watch it? Hunt around for other videos that are along the lines of your topic, looking specifically for the videos that get the most views. Then create a video response to the most popular clips. Ideally, find a clip that has lots of views with no video responses. It's not a guarantee, but it will help to maximize your exposure.

When Arielle Ford was publicist for Deepak Chopra, Wayne Dyer, and many other notables, we had a great thing happen. Dr. Chopra could not make it back in time from India for a feature article in *People* magazine. Arielle called me and asked if I could erase my schedule and devote a week of my life to this article. I immediately accepted, since *People* had a weekly circulation of more than 20 million readers. Johnny Dodd interviewed Jack

Canfield and me over the course of a week. It was intense and exciting. The resulting article was only six paragraphs long (with several excellent photos), but it took our newest book, *A Third Serving of Chicken Soup for the Soul,* to number 1 on the *New York Times* best-seller list.

YouTube viewers can subscribe to your all videos, something you definitely want. Remember I talked earlier about avoiding stagnant content? YouTube is a prime example. If you get subscribers but quit posting videos, you will disappoint them and lose momentum. Make it a goal to post one video a month.

In closing, perfectionism is not your friend on YouTube. In fact, the more organic a video is—with mistakes and all—the more authentic it feels and the more people will relate to it. Some of the most viewed videos on YouTube have never been edited!

This is a useful article on a very basic issue in Internet marketing.

How to Generate Free Traffic to Your Site

by Rick Dearr

Often business owners do not have proficient policies for attracting more people to their web pages, so they instead give these tasks to webmasters and developers, who, if they do it, for the most part do not do it very well. Getting the necessary skills for generating free traffic to your web pages can be vital for realizing your long- and short-term objectives for the business. Some of these solutions can be achieved at a business level, while others may require experts. Most of the techniques for maximizing the number of visitors in a site are free of charge.

You can make use of search utilities to generate more traffic to your site. Visitors access to the sites mostly goes through search engines, such as Google, Yahoo, Exalead, and many more. It is a good practice to optimize your site so that it is easily available through the most popular search engines. There are a myriad ways to achieve this. First, you have to make sure you have the right number of keywords within your site that can draw the citation of most search engines. Other methods could be best applied by a web developer who deals with technical issues, as he has to code tag names and META tags for easier searching.

You can also maximize the number visiting your site by distributing links and adverts for your site at other sites. This is the most appropriate mechanism that businesses owners use to market their products online. Another cheap and affordable method is by exchanging links and advertisements with sites offering similar products to those offered by your site. This will make your website popular amongst potential visitors.

Write and post articles with links to your website to online journals (like e-zines) where people browse to get knowledge on a variety of products. These links should in turn direct the visitors back to more information. Journals that are accessed by thousands of people will increase the chances of making people aware of your site and the products that are offered.

Sites should be friendly and attractive. As a matter of fact, the best sites are designed for the user. You can achieve this by allowing the user to contribute ideas for what they may want from the site. The site should ensure quality. This may include search options or contacts for more information. Whenever the visitor gives his or her views or suggestions, take them as part of the backbone of your site's performance and potential. This drives you to update the site to ensure the traffic is free and efficient. The user will develop a sense of ownership and loyalty to the site.

Here's a good summary of what you need to know about Twitter. Dan Schawbel is the author of *Me 2.0: Build a Powerful Brand to Achieve Career Success.*

Establish a Twitter Marketing Plan

by Dan Schawbel

Just like with any other website or blog, just because you build it doesn't necessarily mean people will come. You should have a marketing plan in place to acquire new followers.

Elements of a Twitter Marketing Plan

- Email signature. You probably already place your blog or website URL and contact information in your email signature, so why not add your Twitter handle? It's free promotion, and every email you send can turn into a new follower.
- Personal or corporate website. If you already have a website for you and/or your company, then you have a platform on which you can promote your Twitter address to people who will probably be interested in following you.
- Blog home page and posts. Your blog is a great place to promote your Twitter account because most people who read blogs know what Twitter is. You should take a two-pronged approach. First, put your Twitter address in one of your sidebars, and second, promote it discreetly in posts every once in a while.

- Email newsletter. If you have an email newsletter, you can write about Twitter and link to your profile or put it at the bottom of your template, so that each email has a link to your account.
- Presentations. Do you do any public speaking? Why not include your Twitter account on the last slide of your presentation and tell people that they can follow you on Twitter?
- Business card. Try including your Twitter handle on your business card. Tony Hsieh of Zappos did this with his card.
- Article writing or guest blog posting. Whenever you write an article for a magazine, news website, or guest post on a blog, try to include your Twitter handle in your byline.
- Networking on Twitter: By using the @ symbol and either retweeting or communicating with other people, you'll have some of them responding to you, thus promoting your Twitter account to many of their followers.
- Promotional products: Somc people take Twitter promotion to the next level. Ted Murphy, for example, created custom shirts that can have your Twitter handle.

Just like with any social network or blog, the more people who follow you, the easier it is to grow your already existing community. Retweets and following other people are two essential ways to get new followers. However, content is king on Twitter, so it is vital to make sure you produce consistent, quality tweets.

ACKNOWLEDGMENTS

I want to acknowledge you, the reader, for reading this book, which I have thoroughly and absolutely enjoyed writing.

Jack Canfield and I were going to write this together once upon a dream, and time and multiple obligations didn't allow it, so I write this version solo and take all the credit and blame personally.

You Have a Book in You! happened because so many curious, creative, interested, wonderful, and loving people have asked me how to write a best seller fast. Of course they added all the little questions in between that I hope I have answered.

What started as an idea and a dream that could potentially serve millions became this book, and it continues as a seminar called "Mega Book Marketing." Why?

Because many brilliant and important books are written and need to be written. If you're interested go to reception @markvictorhansen.com and request information on our next seminar, webinar, podcast, or meeting near you.

Most books will never see the light of day when it comes to readership because of incompetent and inadequate marketing efforts. As I have shown above, 90 percent of the actual process of creating a best seller is, after you have written a great book, backing it up with great marketing.

I am blessed to have interviewed over a hundred supersmart authors—a practice I enjoy and will continue to enjoy for my entire life. I thank each and every one of them for generously giving me and my colleagues their brilliant insights, assurances that you and I can do it, and their vital and heartfelt assistance.

I want to thank Gilles Dana, founder and president of G&D Media, for seeing the potential in this book, because according to a *USA Today* survey, 82 percent of Americans believe they have a book in them. They're right.

I want to serve that market in a great and wonderfully helpful way. We want to see that everyone who writes a book will have a richer and more wonderful and impactful life and lifestyle.

I believe that with Gilles' marketing savvy and innovation we will create ideas, products, services, benefits, and personalities that will help restimulate our economy and get it rocking again.

Mitch Sisskind is my friend and faithful editor and collator par excellence. As a writer himself, Mitch loved this project from the beginning. He took over thirty files of transcribed live audio recordings of everything I had to say about writing over the last twenty years and helped me assemble it into a lucid and hopefully irresistible package. We hope and expect this will motivate you to get your book written, published, and selling ever more briskly.

Richard Smoley, from G&D Media, has done a miraculous job of helping me bring this book completely and comprehensively up to date.

Crystal Dwyer, my sweetheart wife and life partner who generously read, commented on, and thought out loud with me to improve every concept and line in the book—thank you!

To all those who have helped me and whom I neglected to personally or professionally thank and appreciate, I am blessed that you served and aided me in so many ways. Forgive me for not personally naming you and know that I love, thank, and deeply appreciate you.

Allow me again to thank you, the reader, who make it possible for writers to write and earn a life and a great livelihood. I love reading, writing, marketing, selling and that goes into this great process.

I want this book to get ever better. If you have ideas for improving it in future editions, please write me:

Mark Victor Hansen

P.O. Box 27618

Scottsdale, Arizona 85255

Or email me at: reception@markvictorhansen.com, or call

Feel that you are deeply appreciated by me, because you are. If you need someone's permission to write, you now have mine—do an excellent and extraordinary job of writing what desperately needs to be written, because YOU CAN!

The best book of all time hasn't yet been written. So you have to write it!

BONUS
BOOK

HOW TO FAST WRITE A BOOK AND MAKE A FORTUNE

Everything You Need to Know to Write a Book and Get Rich Doing It!

MARK VICTOR HANSEN, ROICE KRUEGER, AND JAMES SKINNER

How to Fast Write a Book and Make a Fortune will show you how to make money from your writing aspirations. You have a book in you!

The Authors

Mark Victor Hansen is the cocreator of the Chicken Soup for the Soul empire and is the best-selling nonfiction author of all time. His goal is to make the planet work for all humanity.

Roice Krueger cofounded Franklin Covey, the world's largest training company, and has supervised consulting projects for 80 percent of the Fortune 500.

James Skinner is the founder of two global financial groups that manage billions of dollars of assets. He is also recognized as one of the world's foremost business thinkers and appears regularly on Japanese television.

Note: Ideas That Can Change Your Life™ is a collaboration of three of the world's most amazing authors, speakers, and thinkers. The first-person "I" in this book may refer to any of the authors.

You Have a Book in You!

You have a book in you! You probably have more than one. But unless you get the words out of you, that's as far as it goes.

The old cliché "Begun is half done" is meant to motivate and inspire us to start things, but it also reminds us that projects we begin and then abandon are of little value.

Books that are only outlined or semiwritten cannot be sold or read.

Decide in the beginning how much time you will dedicate each day or each week to writing, schedule yourself into the process of writing, and then do it.

To Get Started, Begin at the End

To get started, begin at the end—meaning that in your mind's eye, you must see a finished product called a *book*.

Think about what your book will look like when it is done and who will read it.

Whether your book is being written for a general audience for a specific niche, make sure that your target market is big enough and hungry enough for your information and ideas to buy it in quantities that will give you the cash flow that you desire.

The Chicken Soup series are books for a general audience, whereas *How to Make a Fortune in the Carpet Cleaning Business* is a niche-market book.

Decide

Writing a book takes thinking, time, energy, effort, coordination of endless details, and hopefully a team that will support you and participate in the process.

You need to decide to write.

Decide that you are going finish the book.

Decide whether you will write alone or be a coauthor.

Decide whether you want to self-publish, publish electronically, publish with Ideas That Can Change Your Life™ Publishing, or go to a traditional publishing house, such as Penguin Random House, McGraw-Hill, Simon & Schuster, or HarperCollins, to publish, distribute, and sell your book.

Decide what markets you will target and how you will get there.

Some of the big marketplaces include nationwide bookstores (such as Barnes & Noble and Books-A-Million), club stores (Costco, Sam's Club), and major Internet-based distributors (Amazon.com).

Decide whether or not you want to make the effort and pay the price to make your book a best seller.

It can take as much as a year and a half of relentless work to make your dream happen and get to number one on the *New York Times* best-seller list. But the rewards can be well worth it.

If best-seller status is what you're aiming for, either attend Mark's Mega Book Marketing Seminar (held multiple times annually around the world) or get the CDs of his course (go to www.markvictorhansen.com). Mark guarantees that this relatively small investment will give you gigantic returns if you do what it teaches.

Room for Everyone

In 2019, 689.5 million books were sold in America alone—a figure that grows every year.

There is room for everyone.

There is not just one *New York Times* best-seller list but eleven, published every Sunday.

The categories are:

1. Combined print and ebook fiction
2. Combined print and ebook nonfiction
3. Hardcover fiction
4. Hardcover nonfiction
5. Paperback trade fiction
6. Paperback nonfiction

7. Advice, how-to, and miscellaneous
8. Children's middle grade hardcover
9. Children's picture books
10. Children's series
11. Young adult hardcover

Although some readers believe is that there is only 1 *New York Times* Sunday best-selling book a week, you can see that there are 11 lists weekly, each containing either 10 or 15 titles each. This amounts to 140 places per week. If we multiply this by 52 weeks per year, we discover that there are an amazing 7,280 opportunities a year to earn the right to claim that you are a *New York Times* best-selling author. Authors-speakers have almost infinite opportunities, and most start by saying with tongue in cheek, "This is my best seller!"

There is also a national best-seller category of books that have sold more than 20,000 books in a month's time, as recorded by an ever-changing selection of bookstores.

USA TODAY calculates a list of the top 150 best-selling books each week. The first 50 are published in the newspaper, and the top 150 are available online. *USA TODAY*'s list is based on a computer analysis of retail sales nationwide from the previous week.

In the publishing world, there is what is commonly referred to as an "industry rag" (that is, a trade news source) called *Publishers Weekly*, a highly influential publication that features all the industry insiders predicting trends and talking about what's hot and not.

The world book market is even bigger!

This market often buys what America considers the best-sellers, but individual countries can also pick up on their own individual themes.

A quick example is our *Chicken Soup for the Singaporean Soul*, which became the number-one bestseller in Singapore. It sold 20,000 copies during the first week because of phenomenal national pride.

As a 55-year-old country, Singapore is still discovering its own identity. Specialty books alone are 19 percent of the $26.9 billion-a-year business and offer authors total ease of entry, because these books are idea-based.

Only You

A recent *USA TODAY* survey says that 80 percent of Americans want to write a book. There is an infinite number of books that need to be written. You could write one, maybe even more! Your book can ONLY BE WRITTEN BY YOU.

Writing a book gives you influence and mega-credibility, helps expand your reputation, can serve to build your business, and makes a lasting contribution to other people.

Books are like babies: they take on a life of their own as they grow and develop. Best of all, as you write, *you* grow, develop, and become clearer and more focused about what you believe, know, and think.

Also, books carry with them the law of attraction: like-minded people will read them and seek you out for friendship, seminars, coaching, advice, counsel, and partnership.

Writing as Play

Book writing is fun—if you make it fun. Decide that it will be fun for you to write.

Most writers tell themselves it will be laborious, and so it becomes a pain.

We want you to experience and express the joy of writing.

Put yourself in a state of mind in which you love the process. You will be excited to express your highest and best thinking.

Before you start writing, set your intention to have the words flow effortlessly through your fingertips through dictation, pen, pencil, or keyboard.

Writing can be "work-work" or "work-play" or "play-play." The most extraordinary communications will flow through you onto the page once you believe that they will and you make the process "play-play."

We believe and give you permission to believe that this will happen. Get your mind right, and you will write right.

Your Writing Table

Allow us to give you an example of a great best-selling author.

The late Dr. Wayne Dyer showed Mark his writing table. It was an altar to his favorite writers and thinkers, all of whom he wrote about in his book *The Wisdom of the Ages.*

They included thinkers, writers, seers, and sages such as Jesus, Ralph Waldo Emerson, Henry David Thoreau, Lao Tzu, and Sai Baba.

Wayne placed a framed picture of each of these remarkable human beings on what was formerly his kitchen table.

When Wayne was writing a book, his practice was to get up at three or four in the morning to write undisturbed. Wayne had eight children and lived on the beach in Maui, facing the beautiful turquoise-blue waters of the Pacific Ocean.

He used to sit facing the ocean, gently writing on a yellow pad, finishing more than one book each year.

He wrote thirty bestsellers this way!

Born of Desire

You now have a brief idea about potential markets for your book and about a place to write it.

Now it's time to clarify why you want to write it. As you give yourself a big enough reason WHY to write your book, you will guarantee that you will figure out HOW to write it.

Writing starts with the desire to write. You have to want to communicate something to someone.

Jack Canfield and I wanted to write a book (which now has become a series of best sellers consisting of over 250 books) that told heart-touching, soul-penetrating stories.

We received 144 rejections before Health Communications, Inc., in Deerfield Beach, Florida, read our book and said, "We think it might sell 20,000."

As of this writing we have sold 500,000,000 *Chicken Soup* books and our perfect 2029 vision is to have sold one billion books. No one has. I want to be the first. I am busy making it happen in unique, original, and, I believe, inevitable ways. It is great fun.

We wrote the series because at the end of our talks (Mark spoke primarily to business audiences and Jack spoke to education groups), individuals asked each of us if the Bopsy story we spoke about—about a five-year-old boy with leukemia—was in a book. We heard the request often, and the story got a standing ovation every time it was told, so Jack got the idea to do *Chicken Soup for the Soul.*

I asked if we could write it together.

The rest is best-selling history.

How Can You Fast-Write a Book?

So how can you fast-write a book? There are multiple ways.

You can write it yourself.

You can have it ghostwritten.

You can coauthor it.

You can dictate it.

You can interview your way to a book.

You can find someone who has written a great book but has no sales and marketing ability. This person would want you to put your name on it and make the business profits happen, sharing in the revenues that are generated.

You can find public-domain books, write a new preface, foreword, or additional copy, and then recopyright it.

The three of us once dictated over 50 books in just four days in front of a live audience in Southeast Asia.

Get the Brain Storming!

Before you write a book, have a soul-storming session with yourself, friends, or Mastermind group, and write out as many titles as you can.

Include areas of interest you'd like to write about.

Plan to review and add to this list regularly.

When Jack and I started, we once sat in my Jacuzzi for hours and wrote out 137 titles that we thought would be fun, easy, beneficial, wanted by the marketplace, and profitable for us to write.

When we started Ideas That Can Change Your Life™, we brainstormed over 150 different areas that people want to improve and better their lives.

The Secret to Writing Is Writing

We recommend that you write out everything you know about a subject before you start researching it. Just sit down and write it. This approach allows for original thinking and breakthrough ideas.

Write what you know. Surely you have a signature story that you frequently tell to the delight of listeners. Use that to get your mental juices flowing.

To put yourself in a mental state to write, you may take on the persona of your favorite great writer and tap into vibrations of their energy, or you could listen to music that nourishes your creativity. We all love Pachelbel's *Canon in D*, which allows us to write for hours on end.

Don't try to be perfect. Remember, nobody ever publishes their first draft!

A good editor can fix just about anything other than the fact that you haven't written something, so sit down and get started.

Take Bite-Size Chunks

Our friend Bob Proctor, a phenomenal, must-hear speaker and author, once had a woman in his audience say, "I want to write a book, but I don't have time, because I'm married, with four kids, a husband, and a job to go to every day."

"Here is how you do it," said Bob. "*Write one minute every day.* That is a page a day, or 250 words. In one year, you will have written 365 pages. Edit it and you will have finished a book."

She did not take Bob's advice, but he himself did! Bob wrote his first book, *Born Rich*, which has sold millions of copies worldwide, and continues 25 years later to be a *self-promoted and self-published* bestseller.

Author Robert G. Allen says, "Every word I write is worth $20. Therefore my daily writing goal is 1,000 words. The fact that I know I will be exceedingly well paid for my words keeps me disciplined and writing. If I think I want to watch TV but I have not written today, I go to my computer and write."

Mark has coauthored multiple best sellers with Bob Allen—who, by the way, takes financial information that is practically impossible to comprehend and makes it easy for the masses to understand and employ. Bob is a millionaire-maker.

If You Can't Think Book, Think Article

One of Mark's early inspirations was Dr. Jeffrey Lant.

Jeffrey graduated Phi Beta Kappa with a degree in literature from Harvard.

He decided to write money books but instead of starting with the books, he writes content-rich articles on various subjects.

Jeffrey writes two hours a day to complete one content-rich article.

The articles are offered free to small-circulation magazines, of which there are thousands. Their editors are pulling their hair out daily in hopes of finding copy to fill them.

Jeffrey offers his articles free *if* they promise to put his advertising note and email address at the end of the article.

This strategy has garnered Jeffrey more than 650,000 friendly permission-marketed buyers. Jeffrey then turns the same article into a special report, which he sells online for $7.

This is handled by an autoresponder, so he has no hard costs for printing to worry about, no agent, publisher, or anything else—just a money machine.

He compiles those special reports, which sell in the tens of thousands, and turns them into self-published books like *How to Make a Whole Lot More than $1,000,000 Writing, Commissioning, Publishing, and Selling How-to Information.*

Jeffrey then offers these books first to the contacts on his special readers list (who know, love, and trust him) at $40 each.

In the first week he sells over 20,000 copies, which is $800,000! Then he goes to Europe on vacations and invests in art masterpieces.

We share Jeffrey's example because it is a writing, selling, and marketing strategy that you can duplicate, and because it shows you how you can get started by writing articles that later become books.

The whole process is carried out by one person with a computer!

Can you write yourself rich? That is up to you, your dedication, and your passionate purposefulness.

Interviewed by Imagination

Write what you know. You have some information that someone else would love to have. If we could interview you, we could help you discover your special information and turn it into a book right now!

But until we get a chance to interview you in person, take on our personas briefly and pretend we are interviewing you to discover your story, which you will write to make your fortune.

Do you want to write fiction, nonfiction, children's books, romance novels, adventure or travel books, books on fashion, design, art, music, or whatever?

The marketplace is huge and ever growing.

A Publisher on Every Corner

A few decades ago, America had eight big publishers.

With the advent of desktop publishing, that instantly and forever changed.

A company called Ten Speed Press saw a niche to grow rich in.

There were 78 million 10-speed bicycles in America, but no book on how to fix them. They wrote a book on this subject and sold it as a specialty-market book exclusively in bicycle stores; it made them a fast fortune.

Better than that, they opened the floodgates so that others saw a market where none had existed before.

Suddenly 86,000 small publishers and self-publishers came to the marketplace, and each found niche markets hungry for specialty information.

With the advent of Amazon, YouTube, Facebook, and others, the information market is expanding and increasing.

It is hungry for your contributions.

You Can Hire a Ghostwriter

Almost all celebrities and people of fame have ghostwriters who interview them and do the heavy lifting for them in writing their books.

Inexpensive ghostwriters can be found in a multitude of places.

Ask other authors if they know great ghostwriters.

Best-selling novelist James Patterson had a doorman at his high-rise building ask if he could submit something. He became James's top ghostwriter and, now, coauthor.

Every English department head will cheerfully tell you who the students are that have great talent and promise.

In Hollywood, the Screen Writers Guild is loaded and overflowing with talented writers who are hungry for work.

They know the drill—that everything is due yesterday. Most are competent and have plenty of samples to show their skills.

If you come to one of Mark's Mega Book Marketing seminars, you will find so many ghostwriters who have written for famous people that it will astound you.

Online you can seek out ghostwriters at www.elance.com. You decide what you want to say and submit it to Upwork (formerly Elance), a clearinghouse for freelance writers, and you will get inundated with writers that are for hire at unbelievably low prices.

Sample their work before you sign a contract. Many are superb, we are told. You dictate what you want written; they write it, research it, and finish it for you.

Coauthorship Is Wonderfully Beneficial

Coauthorship is another way to get your book out of you and do it fast!

First, it keeps you dedicated to your writing, publishing, and marketing assignments, because you don't want to let down your colleagues, friends, coauthors and future readers.

James, Roice, and I decided to write 100 books in 100 days.

At first blush, the idea seemed ludicrous. As we discussed it and the great benefits of doing it, we got excited. We did everything that we are recommending to you to do. We wrote out hundreds of potential titles. We started at the end: we set a big goal of selling a billion books.

We wanted to reinvent the publishing industry. We wanted to change all the paradigms. We wanted to speed to market. The average book takes two years to write, and often it is obsolete before it gets printed into the light of day. We wanted to communicate what the world needs to hear in a fast way. A book does not need to be 200 pages long when 10, 20, or 30 pages may communicate the entire message effectively and generate the required result.

We thought we could change the price and make more and better information available to millions and potentially billions of readers.

We said we could instantly have our books serving people in 70 languages and in 120 countries the first day they are available.

We would tithe 10 percent of our earnings to causes that we believe in, a practice that Mark launched with the Chicken Soup series.

Ultimately, we would "five- and six-sense" our books so they would get to the readers in the way they want to absorb the information: as text, audio, or video—even olfactorily or by feeling.

We respectfully want to push the edge of your envelope. We want to end illiteracy, poverty, and "have-notness," and we intend to solve many of the world's problems with great information and world-improving ideas.

Our idea is visionary, and as coauthors we want to inspire you to your greatest writing and thinking.

Ralph Waldo Emerson said, "I would rather see a sermon than hear one any day."

As a result of our coauthoring partnership, we wrote 100 books in 95 days, a feat that has never been achieved in the publishing industry anywhere on earth, and we had a tremendous amount of fun doing it!

We hope you SEE our vision, dream, and thinking and are moved to self-reliance and to writing action.

Dictate Your Book

Steve Allen achieved great success as an actor, vocalist, pianist, author, composer, lyricist, and director. He:

- Authored over 50 published books.
- Wrote over 8,500 songs.
- Acted; for example, he had the title role in *The Benny Goodman Story.*
- Wrote for Broadway.
- Was the first host of *The Tonight Show* and is considered the father of TV talk shows.
- Was dyslexic.
- Never had writer's block, because he was working simultaneously on 28 projects at a time. Steve did all of this by dictating into 28 different tape recorders. If he got stalled on one project, he went to work on another, and all got finished.

You can read his inspiring and dynamic story in *Chicken Soup for the Writer's Soul.*

Many would-be great writers don't have the desire to physically write, type, or compute, yet they could master the fine art of dictation.

Again, you can hire a great assistant to transcribe and perfect your dictation.

Another alternative: automatic transcription. The software from Nuance called Dragon claims to have

99 percent accuracy after training. Or you could use www.idictate.com (very inexpensive), and send your dictated files from your computer to theirs in India. Or call your dictation in daily by phone over Skype.com for free.

The possibilities for publishing obviously keep expanding as an increasingly literate world becomes hungry for information, insight, and wisdom.

Put the Experts' Thinking into Books

Interviewing experts is another way to fast-write a book.

This is how Napoleon Hill wrote a book called *Think and Grow Rich*, first published in 1937. It has sold over 100 million copies worldwide. (It is becoming a major motion picture, written by Jim Stovall, the blind author and movie maker of the film *The Ultimate Gift* and many other books and movies. Jim has verbally offered to feature Mark Victor Hansen in the movie.)

Hill interviewed industrialist and philanthropist Andrew Carnegie, and Carnegie liked Hill so much that he tested him. He asked him to invest the next 20 years interviewing the world's 500 best leaders, politicians, and businesspeople. From these he would put together the principles and philosophy of personal success and achievement, and do it as a self-funded author in order to prove that the principles work.

In 30 seconds, Hill agreed. He was later criticized for taking such an assignment from the world's richest man without being paid, but his interviews have helped millions.

You can interview the leaders of any field and instantly turn your material into money-making books, podcasts, virtual seminars, CDs, videos, movies, documentaries, or whatever. As Hill's title says, "Think and grow rich!"

Find a Great Book

Many authors—more than you could possibly believe—have some of the greatest books of all time locked in a safe, file cabinet, file folder, or computer.

Spencer Johnson, MD, wrote a fable after his divorce. Spencer told it as a kids' story again and again to everyone who would listen. He had written *The One Minute Manager* with Dr. Ken Blanchard. Hearing the story, Blanchard told Johnson, "It will be a best seller; let me write the foreword and take you to my agent." The book was called *Who Moved My Cheese?* and has sold over 28 million copies. Johnson needed his buddy to see the enormous value in what he had been sharing as a mere throwaway story, albeit a great one for children.

Why have writers got a backlog of brilliant material hidden away? Because writers write. Prolific writers write prolifically.

Ask writers you meet at Mark's Megas, at Book Expo America, at various writers' meetings and workshops, or at the Maui Writers Conference, and you will find many talented writers with their works, looking for someone to partner with and market them and their book to greatness.

Historically the publishing industry wants only one book from an author every two years. Here are two examples of major writers who wrote more than their publishers would accept and found ways to publish their body of work.

Stephen King had to write under several best-selling pseudonyms.

Nora Roberts told Mark that in longhand she can write 55,000 words a week that are nearly flawless and ready to publish and sell. Nora had to write many bestsellers under the pseudonym J. D. Robb to get her work out and be able to continue to write energetically.

Another way to produce a book is to find books and material in the public domain and reauthor and recopyright them. This is a big business that is little-known.

In the book business, work that was created (fixed in tangible form for the first time) on or after January 1, 1978, is automatically protected from the moment of its creation and is ordinarily given a term enduring for the author's life plus an additional 70 years after the author's death. In the case of "a joint work prepared by two or more authors who did not work for hire," the term lasts for 70 years after the last surviving author's death. This means that (generally speaking) works published over 100 years ago are in the public domain—so anyone can reprint them. Have your attorney check the status of material that you may be interested in adapting to see if it is in the public domain.

In the area of self-help books, Charles "Tremendous" Jones, the late, great author of *Life Is Tremendous*, created the Executive Books Company in Harrisburg, Pennsylvania. Tremendous, as he is affectionately called, rewrote the forewords and introductions to revered classics like James Allen's *As a Man Thinketh* and hundreds of others. He has inspired lots of nonreaders to become readers and is most known for his famous statement: "You will be the same person you are today five years from now except for the books you read, the audios you listen to, and the seminars that you attend."

Charles has sold hundreds of millions of dollars' worth of these books through different means: from his speaking platforms, in volume to major direct-selling companies like Amway, and book by book to his colleague speakers, friends, and customers.

Becoming the Writer You Want to Be

Are you ready to become the writer you want to be, the writer you were born to be, the writer you need to be if others are ever to know what you know?

It is our hope that you will be inspired by the success stories and strategies we have shared to start writing a book that only you can write.

We wish you the best of luck in all your writing pursuits.

Mark Victor Hansen
Roice Krueger
James Skinner

CPSIA information can be obtained
at www.ICGtesting.com
Printed in the USA
LVHW011448070720
659978LV00005B/12

9 781722 502614